\<Other Titles by Will Alexander\>

POETRY

The Audiographic as Data, w/ Carlos Lara (Oyster Moon Press, 2016)
Based on the Bush of Ghosts (Staging Ground, 2015)
The Codex Mirror: 60 drawings - Byron Baker; 60 writings - Will Alexander (Anon Editions, 2015)
Kaleidoscopic Omniscience: Asia & Haiti / The Stratospheric Canticles / Impulse & Nothingness (Skylight Press, 2012)
The Brimstone Boat - For Philip Lamantia (Rêve à Deux, 2012)
Compression & Purity (City Lights, 2011)
The Sri Lankan Loxodrome (New Directions, 2009)
Exobiology As Goddess (Manifest Press, 2005)
Above the Human Nerve Domain (Pavement Saw, 1998)
Asia & Haiti (Sun & Moon, 1995)
The Stratospheric Canticles (Pantograph Press, 1995)
Vertical Rainbow Climber (Jazz Press, 1987)

FICTION

Alien Weaving: Novella (Anonymous Energy, 2016)
Transparent as Witness, w/ Janice Lee (Solar Luxuriance, 2013)
Diary as Sin (Skylight Press, 2011)
Sunrise in Armageddon (Spuyten Duyvil, 2006)
Arcane Lavender Morals (Leave Books, 1994)

BELLES-LETTRES

Secrets Prior To The Sun (White Print Inc, 2016)

PHILOSOPHY

Mirach Speaks to his Grammatical Transparents (Oyster Moon Press, 2011)
Towards the Primeval Lightning Field (O Books, 1998)

ESSAYS

Singing in Magnetic Hoofbeat: Essays, Prose texts, Interviews and a Lecture 1991-2007 (Essay Press, 2012)
On the Substance of Disorder (Insert Press, 2011)
Inalienable Recognitions (eohippus labs, 2010)

DRAMA

At Night On the Sun (Chax Press, 2016)
Inside the Earthquake Palace: 4 Plays (Chax Press, 2011)

\< Also from Rêve à Deux \>

Sotère Torregian *Surreal Adventurer*, 2015
Marie Wilson & Nanos Valaoritis *Land of Diamond*, 2015
Sotère Torregian *The Age of Gold (Redux)*, 2012
Will Alexander *The Brimstone Boat - For Philip Lamantia*, 2012
Schlechter Duvall *The Adventures of Desirée*, 2009

Spectral Hieroglyphics

WILL ALEXANDER
Spectral Hieroglyphics

A Poetic Troika

★ ★ ★

Illustrated by
RIK LINA
&
Prologue by
Laurens Vancrevel

Rêve à Deux

Los Angeles - Amsterdam - Vacaville

Copyright © 2016 by Will Alexander

The cover design is by Richard Waara.
Thom Burns provided invaluable creative assistance.

Back cover & frontispiece photographs (page 7) of
"Will Alexander at *Beyond Baroque*, Venice, CA 2016"
© by Raman Rao.

Almost the entirety of the artwork in this book is
profusely illustrated (other than when noted)
by & © by Rik Lina.

Rêve à Deux would like to thank James Brook
for his redacting assistance on the *Prologue*.

Rêve à Deux

Rêve à Deux was founded in 2009, and is edited by Richard Waara.
Additional paperback copies of this book, and other
Rêve à Deux titles, are available on Amazon.com or Lulu.com.
Hardback editions of some of our titles are available
exclusively at: http://www.lulu.com
This individual title has a Black & White Paperback Edition and
a Color Paperback Edition.

ISBN 978-0-578-18092-2 (Black & White Paperback Edition);
ISBN 978-0-578-18093-9 (Color Paperback Edition)

BLACK & WHITE PAPERBACK EDITION

Printed in the United States of America

CONTENTS

Drawing: "Dragon Days" by Rik Lina...ii-iii

Frontispiece (Title Page): "Le Jet de sang (for Antonin Artaud)," Drawing by Rik Lina.. 1

Contents.. 4

Frontispiece (Prologue): "Will Alexander at Beyond Baroque, Venice, CA 2016," Photograph by Raman Rao.. 7

PROLOGUE:
Some Introductory Observations on Will Alexander's *Spectral Hieroglyphics* by Laurens Vancrevel.. 8

Asemic Drawing I by Rik Lina... 21

THE ONE TRUE BODY, for Antonin Artaud by Will Alexander........................... 22

/Cubomania ("Slash cubomania"): "Antonin Artaud" by Richard Waara................. 23

Drawing: Left half of "Dragon Days" by Rik Lina.. 31

Drawing: Right half of "Dragon Days" by Rik Lina.. 44

Drawing: Left half of "Black Horizon" by Rik Lina... 55

Drawing: Right half of "Black Horizon" by Rik Lina... 68

Asemic Drawing II by Rik Lina... 75

Antonin Artaud: A Glossary of Fumes by Will Alexander.................................... 76

Asemic Drawing III by Rik Lina.. 81

AT THE VERTIGO BORDERS, for Roger Gilbert-Lecomte by Will Alexander...... 82

/Cubomania: "Roger Gilbert-Lecomte" by Richard Waara.................................... 83

Automatic Drawing I by Rik Lina... 90

Automatic Drawing II by Rik Lina... 102

Automatic Drawing III by Rik Lina.. 113

Automatic Drawing IV by Rik Lina.. 125

Automatic Drawing V by Rik Lina... 136

Automatic Drawing VI by Rik Lina.. 145

Asemic Drawing IV by Rik Lina... 155

Glossary for AT THE VERTIGO BORDERS... 156
Asemic Drawing V by Rik Lina... 161
ON HIGHER PHLOGISTON CURRENT, for Aimé Césaire by Will Alexander.... 162
/Cubomania: *"Aimé Césaire"* by Richard Waara....................................... 163
Automatic Drawing VII by Rik Lina.. 173
Automatic Drawing VIII by Rik Lina... 183
Automatic Drawing IX by Rik Lina... 192
Drawing: "The Wind from Nowhere" by Rik Lina...................................... 201
Automatic Drawing X by Rik Lina.. 211
Automatic Drawing XI by Rik Lina... 221
Glossary for *On Higher Phlogiston Current*.. 222
Drawing: "Portrait of a Musician" by Rik Lina.. 232
Drawing: "Black Horizon" by Rik Lina.. 233

For Clayton Eshleman
who paved the way for me into print.

Will Alexander at *Beyond Baroque*, Venice, CA 2016   Photo by Raman Rao

Some introductory observations on Will Alexander's *Spectral Hieroglyphics* by Laurens Vancrevel

Will Alexander's three long poems—"The One True Body," "At the Vertigo Borders," and "On Higher Phlogiston Current," which constitute the "poetic troika" *Spectral Hieroglyphics*—are dedicated to the lives and works of three exceptional francophone poets of the first half of the twentieth century: Antonin Artaud (1896-1948), Roger Gilbert-Lecomte (1907-1943), and Aimé Césaire (1913-2008), who opened new horizons in poetry and the philosophy of life.

Yet "dedicated" is perhaps too restrictive a word to characterize the thrust of Alexander's poems. At first, each poem seems to be an imaginary conversation as well as a profound self-analysis of the poet in the light of the works and aspirations of their subjects. The three poems of *Spectral Hieroglyphics* are, however, more like odes to kindred spirits who have dared to revolutionize poetic expression and who have created astonishing visionary images in a highly personal language.

Spectral Hieroglyphics is, in all of these aspects, a continuation of Alexander's previous investigations into the freedom of the poet, including his first long poem dedicated to a fellow writer, "The Brimstone Boat,"[1] which focuses on Philip Lamantia, and the more recent "Based on the Bush of Ghosts,"[2] in which the Nigerian author Amos Tutuola serves as the fulcrum.

★   ★   ★

Alexander's poetic mentor, Philip Lamantia—that magnificent innovator of the content and tone of American poetry—courageously freed his work from the constraints of conventional moral elegance by imbuing it with the spirit of revolt and the flame of the marvelous. In an essay on Lamantia, Alexander writes: "I was always listening to him in my mind, and so when I met him face to face it was a twelve hour encounter which has marked me forever."[3] "The Brimstone Boat" is a continuation of this first encounter and an ode to the poetic hero who was to become an unforgettable friend.

In a short essay in homage to Lamantia, "Philip Lamantia: Perpetual Incandescence,"[4] Alexander notes that Lamantia had received "the password from a magus," that is to say, from André Breton, the main philosopher and arbiter of surrealism, who had found in Lamantia's early poems "a voice that rises once in a hundred years." For Alexander, Lamantia was the embodiment of total liberation in the quest for the marvelous. In the same essay, which is included in *Singing in Magnetic Hoofbeat*, Alexander writes:

> …Philip Lamantia palpitates, poem after poem, book after book, like quantum spiraling, intermittent, oblique, fueled by the sun of interjacence. Not the sun as furnace, but light as transformative eternity.
> And it was this great personal fire which first dazzled me about Lamantia. His works became my cryptic ritual criteria…[5]

Tutuola, the African master of visionary storytelling, appealed to Alexander's imagination in a very different way. The stories in *My Life in the Bush of Ghosts* (1954) evoke the escape of a young boy into the ominous jungle after slave traders entered his village. The young wanderer discovers the marvels of an animistic universe in which spirits of the woods protect him. *My Life in the Bush of Ghosts* is a salutary allegory of the aspiration to a new society—a society that repels exploitation and organized looting by creating a world without slavery and colonialism, a society that strives for spiritual unity and cooperation. In "Based on the Bush of Ghosts," Alexander addresses Tutuola:

> Amos
>
> […] *as animist you know that nothing could be quarantined*
>
> *that nothing could be conveyed*
>
> *to the torrentially gangrenous*
>
> *to the Western finance model*[6]

The finance model of the Western world and its globalized so-called free market are seen as the reincarnation of the old colonial system and its many forms of slavery. Alexander's poetry expresses a revolt against these contemporary, invisible slave drivers.

★   ★   ★

In contradiction to the prevailing, contemporary pursuit of solitary self-interest, the three poets presented in *Spectral Hieroglyphics* defended human emancipation and freedom of expression.

They inscribed their visions in beautiful but shocking poetry, exhibiting the kind of radical beauty that Breton called "convulsive." Because of this, their work has served as a profound inspiration to Alexander's own work, notwithstanding the dissimilarity of their poetic registers.

Both Artaud and Gilbert-Lecomte were *poètes maudits*, accursed poets, who created their works as if standing on the rim of a spiritual volcano as they rebelled against the constraints of bourgeois society with its moral codes. Among their precursors are Edgar Allan Poe, William Blake, and Friedrich Hölderlin as well as the most famous *poètes maudits* of nineteenth-century French literature: Gérard de Nerval, Charles Baudelaire, Lautréamont, and Arthur Rimbaud, forerunners of the early twentieth-century literary avant-garde.

Césaire, the third poet of the troika, was not a *poète maudit* but a spiritual freedom fighter for the black communities in the French Commonwealth both in his visionary poetry and in his political activity. Breton was one of the first to appreciate Césaire's poetry, together with that of Artaud and Gilbert-Lecomte. In a 1946 interview, he said in connection with their works:

> In order to fight the mortal boredom that is distilled nowadays by many so-called poetry publications, the accent should be shifted to the power of excess that creates both movement and freedom.[7]

★   ★   ★

Artaud, essentially an extrovert, always urged his audiences to push back frontiers. When he directed the Bureau for Surrealist Research from 1924 to 1925, he gave public consultations on dreams, poetry, and surrealism. In 1926, he co-founded the Théâtre Alfred Jarry in order to bring his ideas on the "theater of cruelty" into the limelight. In *Le Théâtre et son double* (The Theater and Its Double, 1938), he pleads for a radically different "total theater" in which entertainment is abolished. (Judith Malina and Julian Beck's Living Theater was based on Artaud's ideas.)

Alexander writes on Artaud in his essay "Alchemy as Poetic Kindling":

> [Artaud] sought a thrilling catharsis existence for both performance and audience as one unbroken flaw. He desired an inhabited theatre, an impalpable poetic theatre. Instead, what he confronted was theatre as a fort for legal entertainment, to be forgotten on entering the boulevard. What Artaud called for was a poetics of thirst, a striving for greater existence.[8]

Not only a poet and an innovator of the theater, Artaud also acted in films and delivered sensational addresses at the University of Paris at the request of René Allendy, a professor of psychiatry. From his early years, he suffered from unbearable neuralgic pains that were relieved by opiates, to which he became addicted; this addiction caused many physical disorders and ultimately severe psychosis. In the late 1930s, he was treated in a psychiatric hospital, where he was administered the then new therapy of electroshock—a gruesome experience.

Artaud was radically critical of modern Western culture and institutionalized religions. He aimed at an entirely different vision of life, which he hoped to find among the indigenous peoples of Mexico and the surviving Celtic beliefs in Ireland as he traveled to these countries to observe ancient rituals and traditional customs. He stayed for a long time with the Tarahumara Indians in northern Mexico, where he shared their peyote ritual, writing of them in his still timely book:

> If magic is a constant communication from the inner self directed to exterior reality, from the act to thought, from things to words, from matter to spirit, we can say that we have lost this flashing inspiration, this form of nervous illumination, long ago, and that we need to bathe once more in living, untainted springs. For a very long time, there have been no myths in Europe in which people can believe in. We all need to look for the birth of a valid and collective myth.[9]

Artaud had a profound interest in the ancient writings of Asia as well as other sources of such a new myth. Alexander looks to Artaud the visionary poet in his "The One True Body":

> *your discourse*
>
> *strife*
>
> *your modes & operation*
>
> *a stark incendiary rebus*
>
> . . . .
>
> *you*
>
> *blemished shaman as fever*
>
> *as energy though fluidic mesmerizing screens*

After three years in the mental hospital of Rodez in the South of France, Artaud reappeared in Paris in January 1947, wrecked by drugs and electroshock treatment. To provide him with the means for private care, his friends organized a fundraising event in the small Théâtre du Vieux Colombier, where Breton gave the welcoming speech:

> In a different society, less pervaded by rationality, Artaud would be a shaman, because he has been able to pass to the reverse side of the mirror, and he has seen what is not given to us to know.[10]

Artaud himself delivered a most impressive and spirited speech, "The Lived History of Artaud-Mômo," which was published shortly after the event.

During the last year of his life, Artaud feverishly wrote poems, essays, and other texts that filled hundreds of school notebooks. In 1947, his long poem "Van Gogh le suicidé de la société" (Van Gogh, the Man Suicided by Society) appeared, a moving cry from the heart on the solitude of the doomed visionary creator and a violent attack on the psychiatric treatment of psychosis. Many other poets have adapted the free structure of that poem, which may also have inspired Alexander.

Also in 1947, the Office de Radiodiffusion Française commissioned Artaud to write a radio poem, without any restriction on the contents. The result was the visionary text of *Pour en finir avec le jugement de dieu* (To Have Done with the Judgement of God), which was recorded with the voices of well-known actors Maria Casarès, Paule Thévenin, and Roger Blin as well as that of Artaud himself. But the day before the announced broadcast, the ORF's director general prohibited it with a charge of blasphemy. A nationwide public scandal resulted, with vehement polemics between liberal Parisian intellectuals and the Catholic establishment. Artaud decided to publish his text at once, but he died from an overdose of painkillers before the book came off the press in early 1948.

Artaud's poetry and essays have had a far-reaching significance for new literature and theater in France and elsewhere, even if his goal of inciting a radical, essential renewal of life and art was not achieved.[11] In "The One True Body," Alexander expresses empathy for the risks Artaud took in pursuit of his lofty mission:

> *A dialogue provoked by your works*
>
> *provoking in me a need to clamber the steps of your suicidal reason*
>
> *ignited in me the viciousness of study*
>
> . . . .
>
> *I could never call your reason*

a terse or criminal fantasia

but simply call it a true implosional roaming

all the while rising through crossing & recrossing mis-supported planks

. . . . .

for me

the morphine was a sigil

an immense green buzzing

always covering your true ignition.

★   ★   ★

Gilbert-Lecomte was very different: he could be called introverted and shy, even if his visionary ideas had great affinity with Artaud's. A brilliant youngster, he founded a poets' group with René Daumal and Pierre Minet, fellow pupils at his high school. This group of friends would later evolve into the avant-garde group Le Grand Jeu, which had a close relationship with the surrealist group around André Breton. (In French, *le grand jeu* designates the full tarot deck.) Irreconcilable views on political commitment between the two groups precluded their union, though they held each other in high esteem. Breton remembered "the very vivid affinities between us that I felt from the beginning." In 1948, he wrote that Gilbert-Lecomte was the "great poet of knowing, creating at the same time a high-tension lyricism."[12]

From adolescence on, Gilbert-Lecomte suffered from frighteningly depressive moods. He was treated with morphine, to which he became addicted, an addiction that slowly ruined his life—physically and materially. He died in a coma at age thirty-six from a tetanus infection caused by an unclean needle. In this context, Alexander makes a moving comparison with Artaud in "At the Vertigo Borders":

you were not unlike Artaud

spun in a zone between

personality & its absence

One of Gilbert-Lecomte's early essays has the rather suicidal title "Monsieur Morphée empoissonneur public" (Mr. Morpheus the Public Poisoner, 1930), a text notable for its "doomed" message. In his periods of vitality between depressions, Gilbert-Lecomte was a frenetic writer not only of lengthy letters to his friends but also of unusual experimental poetry and daring essays. Alexander evokes these writings as "the penetrant sound of an unceasing river through 'toxicomania.'"

Gilbert-Lecomte's first publication was the strong preface/manifesto of the journal *Le Grand Jeu*, which appeared in the summer of 1928; it begins with these words:

> Le Grand Jeu is irreparable: this game is played just once and no more. We want to play the game every moment of our lives. It is a matter of 'the loser is the winner' because we aim to pour out all of ourselves. We want to win. Le Grand Jeu is a game of chance, that is to say: a game of skill, or better yet: a game of luck…

A few months later, the second issue featured his essay "Arthur Rimbaud—la mort des arts" (Arthur Rimbaud: Death of the Arts), which caused a lively discussion in the avant-garde circles of Paris. Gilbert-Lecomte was invited to introduce the collected letters of Rimbaud, published in 1929, establishing him as a major new voice in poetry.

When Gilbert-Lecomte's first book of poetry, *La Vie, l'amour, la mort, le vide et le vent* (Life, Love, Death, the Void, and the Wind), appeared in 1933, Artaud wrote an admiring review in which he praised his exceptional poetic voice:

> Roger Gilbert-Lecomte is one of the rare poets of our time who cultivates a violent, knotty, scorching lyricism, the lyricism of the cries of a flayed being, displaying abrupt words, forced images in which convulsion and spasm render the sounds of nature in the midst of childbirth.[13]

In 1937, a small second book of poetry appeared, *Le Miroir noir* (The Black Mirror); its penultimate poem, "Testament," opens with "I come from afar much farther away / Than people might imagine."

Gilbert-Lecomte became deeply involved in the esoteric and antirational traditions of Europe and Asia while remaining a militant adversary of all religions. In his essays, he defended the fact that, next to the universality of science and mathematics, the equally important universality of other domains of the mind should be recognized, such as those of dreams and myths, fields where metamorphosis is a central quality—and also the domain of mystic experience, that of the visionary, by which the state of ecstasy can be reached. Gilbert-Lecomte held that the domain of mysticism had been unjustly monopolized and deformed by religions. To quote from one of his essays, transcribed from manuscripts and edited by Arthur Adamov in the posthumous book *Testament* (1955):

> The point is to provide the rational and scientific culture of modern man with the basis, the foundations, the roots, its ancient inspiration, its wild spirit of dialectical monism that wipes out all antinomies (matter/mind, dream/reality, etc.), with its sense of symbols and analogies, of rituals and universal myths that unite man with heaven. Just that is the immense task of those whom I call poets, creators, prophets. Alone, in the avant-garde of the human mind, they struggle at 'the borders of the boundlessness and the future.' [14]

A few of his many essays appeared in literary journals during his lifetime, but most of his work was published posthumously. While his collected works finally appeared in 1974, the radical writings of Gilbert-Lecomte have never reached the general public; he remains "a writers' writer."[15]

★   ★   ★

Aimé Césaire was not a *poète maudit*, but he was just as much a militant, courageous innovator of language and poetry. As a principled politician, he spurred the emancipation of the black communities of the former French colonies. He was also the author of a small but impressive body of poetry and drama.

Césaire was "discovered" as a unique poet by Breton in 1941, and they remained friends ever after. Alexander recognizes Césaire's spiritual emancipation by poetry in his own aspirations, as evidenced in his essay "A New Liberty of Expression":[16]

> As Césaire has pointed out, surrealism sparked the African in him. And I can say much the same, in that it has liberated my animistic instinct, so that I am able with unlimited range to roam throughout my writing.

Césaire was born in what was then the French colony of Martinique, a small island in the Lesser Antilles in the eastern Caribbean Sea, whose economy was based on sugar plantations. A promising student, Césaire was selected to receive a high school education in Paris at the prestigious *Lycée Louis-le-Grand* before moving on to the *École Normale Supérieure*, the elite institution for training French civil servants. At the Lycée Louis-le-Grand, among his fellow pupils was Léopold Senghor, later to become the first president of Senegal when that country achieved independence from France. It was Senghor who informed Césaire about the colonial setup in French Africa and the true position of the black population, driving home to him what needed to be done in order to achieve black emancipation.

At the École Normale Supérieure, Césaire encountered a group of black surrealist and communist students, among whom were the young poets Étienne Léro and René Ménil. In 1932, they had published a proud black manifesto against colonialism, *Légitime défense* (Self-Defense), which was accompanied by their essays and poems. This manifesto started the *nègritude* movement, a movement of black cultural awareness in the French Commonwealth, which made a great impression on Césaire, inspiring him as to write his long poem of black revolt, *Cahier d'un retour au pays natal* (Notebook of a Return to the Native Land). Although rejected by a leading French publishing house, the poem appeared in the literary journal *Volontés* in 1938, but passed unnoticed. In 1939, having obtained his degree as a qualified teacher, Césaire returned to Martinique, where he found a teaching job.

With René Ménil and other young Martinicans, Césaire founded the literary journal *Tropiques* (Tropics) to give the new progressive generation its own voice, presenting their poetry and essays to the very conservative colonial island.

While en route from occupied France to the United States (where he was accepted as an refugee from Nazi-dominated Europe) in April 1941, André Breton arrived by boat at Fort-de-France, Martinique's capital, where he and his family had to wait for a connecting ship to New York City. There as he sought a hair ribbon for his young daughter Aube in a grocer's shop, he found the first issue of *Tropiques* on display and leafed through it. Césaire's introductory note aroused Breton's interest with its poetic self-awareness. When he asked the shopkeeper if she knew Césaire, she replied that Césaire was a friend and that she was René Ménil's sister. She promised to tell Césaire that Breton wanted to meet him.

The next day, Aimé and Suzanne Césaire invited Breton to meet in what turned out to be a mutually inspiring encounter. Césaire suggested that Breton contribute to the next issue of *Tropiques*, which led to a series of Breton's prose poems about his stay on Martinique appearing in later issues of the journal. Césaire also presented Breton an offprint of the 1938 publication of his *Cahier d'un retour au pays natal*, which excited Breton both by its powerful message of black awareness and its unorthodox poetic structure. In his essay on Césaire, "Un grand poète noir" (A Great Black Poet), Breton described the text as "a poem having a theme and a stand."

Thanks to Breton's mediation, *Cahier d'un retour au pays natal* appeared in Paris in 1947, with Breton's essay as a preface.[17] Breton called the poem "nothing less than the greatest lyrical monument of our times."[18] He also wrote a beautiful work on his stay, *Martinique, charmeuse des serpents* (Martinique, Snake Charmer), published in 1948 in Paris, in which he describes the wonderful encounter with the Césaires and their friends but also the racist and hypernationalistic behavior of the colonial authorities.

Césaire's *Cahier* may also have prompted Breton to write his own poem "having a theme and a stand." During the summer of 1945, he and Elisa Bindorff, a Chilean pianist, traveled through Nevada, Arizona, and New Mexico. (They married in Nevada, where the ceremony could be performed on short notice.) Breton carried in his luggage the collected works of the utopian philosopher Charles Fourier (bought in an antiquarian bookshop in New York), which were inspiration for his *Ode à Charles Fourier*, begun during the trip. Breton used the poem's colloquial tone and its broad social vista as new ways to express philosophical and political ideas in poetry.

After the war and Martinique's transformation into an overseas department of France in 1945, Césaire was elected mayor of Fort-de-France and deputy to the French General Assembly for the island. He had the support of the French Communist Party, who were practically the only allies of the black equal rights movement in the former colonies. In 1956, however, Césaire resigned from the Party in protest against the Stalinist supremacy within the party and its policy of "socialist realism." In an open letter to the former surrealist Louis Aragon, who served on the board of the Party, Césaire expressed his immense disappointment with communism. At this time, he also published his manifesto *Discours sur le colonialisme* (Discourse on Colonialism), which he dedicated "To André Breton, from whom I was separated by some temporary circumstances, with the assurance of my loyalty to the essential things, of which he always has been the most qualified interpreter." That same year, Césaire founded the Progressive Party of Martinique, which he presided over until his death in 2008.

One of the staunchest defenders of equal rights in the francophone world, Césaire was also one of its most original poets.[19] Alexander acknowledges his unique poetic voice and his political courage in "On Higher Phlogiston Current":

> *Aimé*
>
> *a blue uranian breathing*
>
> *an unnamed flight by agreement*
>
> *such are your poems*
>
> *with their nitric shifts*
>
> *with their cellular wisdom*
>
> *. . . . .*
>
> *because our eyes can see through African solar foil*
>
> *we are privy to solar codex fountains*
>
> *to igniferous hurricanes by sign*

*   *   *

In this extraordinary troika of poems, Alexander not only reveals the strong determination of three free minds to achieve a fully poetic way of life, he also demonstrates the actuality of their revolutionary visions. He transfers these often shocking but always emancipating visions which originated in the first half of the twentieth century to a new age—to our time in which such uncompromising ideas are generally discouraged. He admits that all three poets sacrificed a life without cares to their risky aspirations. Artaud and Gilbert-Lecomte in fact gave their lives for their radical poetry; both suffered precarious physical conditions worsened by addiction to drugs. As a young man, Césaire gave priority to his social and political idealism during a crucial moment in history while neglecting his exceptional literary talents. Alexander portrays these poets in the grandeur of their passionate ideas.

Spectral Hieroglyphics is a timeless "organic constellation" of automatic writing on the unstoppable power of radical poetic vision, if I may repeat that qualifying phrase which Alexander applied to his other major poetic trilogy, *Kaleidoscopic Omniscience*[20]—that tense constellation of poems on the destructive psychosis of the abuse of power, on the one hand, and the healing mystery of the cosmos, nature, and art, on the other. Artaud's path of alchemical transmutation from everyday banality to the desired gold of imagination and passion passes through the shocking acts of the theater of cruelty. Gilbert-Lecomte's experimentation with the summits of consciousness that then converge with abysses indicates the solitary path to unlimited freedom. And Césaire's discovery of the phlogiston of the mind, the invisible spirit of fire, which is hidden in every human being, will lead eventually to the radical emancipation of everyone. Alexander revives these visions in a new myth for the future.

April 27, 2016

Notes

1. Will Alexander, *The Brimstone Boat. For Philip Lamantia. Poetry & Essays.* Rêve à Deux: Los Angeles, San Francisco, Vacaville, 2012. The poem "The Brimstone Boat" first appeared in print in *Faucheuse 3* in 2000.

2. Will Alexander, *Based on the Bush of Ghosts.* Stage Press: New York City, 2015.

3. Will Alexander, *Singing in Magnetic Hoofbeat: Essays, Prose texts, Interviews and a Lecture, 1991-2007.* Essay Press: Ithaca NY, 2012, p. 110

4. In: *Singing in Magnetic Hoofbeat*, p. 109.

5. *Singing in Magnetic Hoofbeat*, p. 110.

6. *Based on a Bush of Ghosts*, p. 6.

7. André Breton, *Entretiens* (edition of 1973), p. 245.

8. In: *Singing in Magnetic Hoofbeat*, p. 149.

9. Antonin Artaud, *Vie et mort de Satan le Feu*, Éditions Arcanes: Paris, 1953, pp. 57-58.

10. André Breton, "Hommage à Antonin Artaud", in: *La Clé des champs*, 1967, p. 166.

11. The most reliable English language anthology of Artaud's works is: *Antonin Artaud, Selected Writings*, translated by Helen Weaver, with an introduction by Susan Sontag. Artaud's book of essays on the theatre, *The Theatre and Its Double*, has been translated by Mary Caroline Richards, and published in 1958 by Grove Weidenfeld: New York.

12. In the surrealist journal *Néon* No. 2 (1948).

13. In: *Nouvelle Revue Française*, No. 255 (1934).

14. Roger Gilbert-Lecomte, *Testament*. Gallimard: Paris 1955, p. 87.

15. Translations into English of a small selection of the works by Gilbert-Lecomte are available at the internet site www.rogergilbertlecomte.com. Recent books in English on Le Grand Jeu: René Daumal & Roger Gilbert-Lecomte: *Theory of the Great Game*, Atlas Press: London, 2015; Roger Gilbert-Lecomte, *The Book is a Ghost*, Solar Luxuriance: San Francisco, 2015.

16. *Singing in Magnetic Hoofbeat*, p. 136.

17. In January of 1947 Brentano's, New York, published a French version of *Cahier* based on a 1942 revision, along with an English translation. In March a substantially revised version, done four years later, is published in Paris by Bordas. André Breton wrote the prefaces for both books. Refer to: Aimé Césaire, *The Original 1939 Notebook of a Return to the Native Land*, Wesleyan University Press: Middleton, Conn., 2013.

18. Included in: André Breton, *Martinique: Charmeuse de serpents*. Paris, 1948.

19. The practically complete poetry by Aimé Césaire has been translated into English by Clayton Eshleman and Annette Smith: *Aimé Césaire, The Collected Poetry*, University of California Press, 1983. See Note 17, for instance, for other published versions of *Cahier*. Also, Aimé Césaire, *Solar Throat Slashed: The Unexpurgated 1948 Edition*, translated and edited by A. James Arnold and Clayton Eshleman, Wesleyan University Press: Middleton, Conn., 2012. All the original French poems *en face* with new English translations.

20. Will Alexander, *Kaleidoscopic Omniscience*, Skylight Press: Cheltenham, 2013. This trilogy combines the books *Asia & Haiti*, *The Stratospheric Canticles* and *Impulse & Nothingness*. The last title appears here in print for the very first time.

The One True Body

"...I have found that in Artaud
the ancient black springs of poetry
are graspable..."

–Clayton Eshleman

Antonin Artaud

for Antonin Artaud

And you've said it throughout living eternity
that the one true body is the condoned & tortured forge
is the bottomless Aleph
is the dazzling obturation
by incontestable stealth
by rumour as dormition
as volcanic dossier
as staggered epistle free falling in flames

I'm looking behind you in mirrors
which suck your flames from the sea
& you know this
by continuing to listen to these ghosts in my diction
not as nervous imposture
but by someone insisting on your form as armada

& this armada now brews through the form that you held
& now insists on itself as alchemical carnage
all the while speaking through crows
through ventriloquial anacondas

& you
you by your anti-induction
understood through your fissures
the dynamics endemic to both serpent & crow

You remain to us all
the sculpted antagonist

pressure through deafening intention
& as result
your zodiac remains shifted with navamshas which incinerate
which then take as their result
the black remarks from ocular curses
arising from counter ostentation
so as to take on devolved statistics
of the shopkeeper's resumes & debits

& Antonin this remains your voice
clashing against stadia
even in death seeking to possess your various momentums
the plagues you brought to bear
according to the cells which evolved from the moons in your
    anti-cryptography

I can never give dates to these moons
or thread by caliper
the threat which conjoined with your contorted biography
on each cold day
of the bells you rang in your psychic cellar
were signs
treacherous enigmas
neon remains
during a pointless germinal hour

& as you knew
at certain hours of the day
carnivorous phlogiston would cast itself through bad civic magic
casting

across a reversed storm of rays
understood as such through divination by destruction

There was superimposition & worry
which you would declare and repeat
declare & repeat
by means of devastating emphatics
being something outside calumny & umber
being something outside the dodecahedral
sparked by doused lightning rods

& these lightning rods were salt
which you saw as peculiar shadows through apparition
through transparent edict

& as one apparition to another
I understand your anger at pointless yield
of the capital markets
of the futility of Marxist labour
being trace or purported evil as fumes across the human electrical
    field
rife with conflagration
according to the notions of oriental fungi

This for you
was not an anodyne mural
but pointed to you in your ire
as a stark implosional critic
bent as you were on creating the fuels of hell
gnawing like a creature on alchemic exhibit

Yet you were not the negated doctor
sequestered by fumes by means of legendary withdrawal

Not partially ignited gemstone
condemned to a purposeless foundry
as connoisseur empebbled by motionless grasp
mingled with the theatric through superficial confusion

You were not on the boulevard
with your body on fire
just to have your body on fire
so as to instruct passersby
with salt through rapacious anagrams

Never the felicitous as sanction
or as microbial or accessible witness

Again
never the leakage of miracles
where you expelled a diamond intact
claiming it was a substance
as a transfixed rosary by decay

As object
seemingly condensed by exterior nostrum
form in this sense being a volcanic mystagogue
being a truncated ruby
not unlike a curious Thracian chamber gone awry in a mollified
    Herculaneum
yet within this ruby a motionless visible body transpired
clouded with spectres from egregious mausoleums

Yet you
the hounded night spirit
was always waking up as a form in blurred vicinities
knowing your partial biology as Greek
as prone to amoeba
again
as partial anthracite as source

This is what I consider as your personal restoration as orbit
as ulterior instigation
not unlike a dazed swimming
over & beyond predetermined mountain peaks
never prone to simulation as rote by calligraphy

This may in time give us name
in the guise of unsaturated fuel

& you perhaps
the true incursion of this fuel
being sigil as perfect flank in the mind
through a strange atomic postern
always posing to your self as a chromosomal riddle

Yet it was something more like a mist
where barriers congealed & reopened
where sounds were broken
where the Sun was truly shifted in itself

Thereby understanding
the open gladioli as bluish invicta

as holding vacuum
thereby
sketching with the voice arcane modes & apparitions

Again
you were audition by confounding
by stupor which ignited from scorching carrion liquor
which subsisted by means of sequestered ambulation
always speaking on behalf of those who were perpetually contested
who were phyla sustained in biological gullies
in ghostly dromedary leavings

Certainly not a stark or sequential production
or an origami of canons
or the power to deproject uplifting

Again
not façade
nor the power which dwells by embellishment
but depth by brutish squalls
by akashic indemnification
under the torch of your foundering vocal emissions
like a moth
seemingly monomial
which fluttered in your bones like a cryptic distillation

Thus
the body at its core

Thus

the body at the core of spillage & errata
notorious with zealotic intangibles
soldered with unsettling prisms

Thus the goal of your body was drought
was decomposed flame
was the multidimensional as study

So over & over by waking compunctious mass
there was fury
there was the in-sovereign as fury
over layered with fury
advanced beyond betrayal
through both scorched & eroded identity

This was the juncture of your resource as fever
as a series of juggled adders
hissing in the background as a broken or secluded storm
as multiple
writhing
the absolute opposite of misanthropic sterility

I'm thinking of the bones you projected in a previous era
awkward
stumbling
unpresentable as regards the bourgeoisie & its ethers
always challenging the rules of self-exhibit

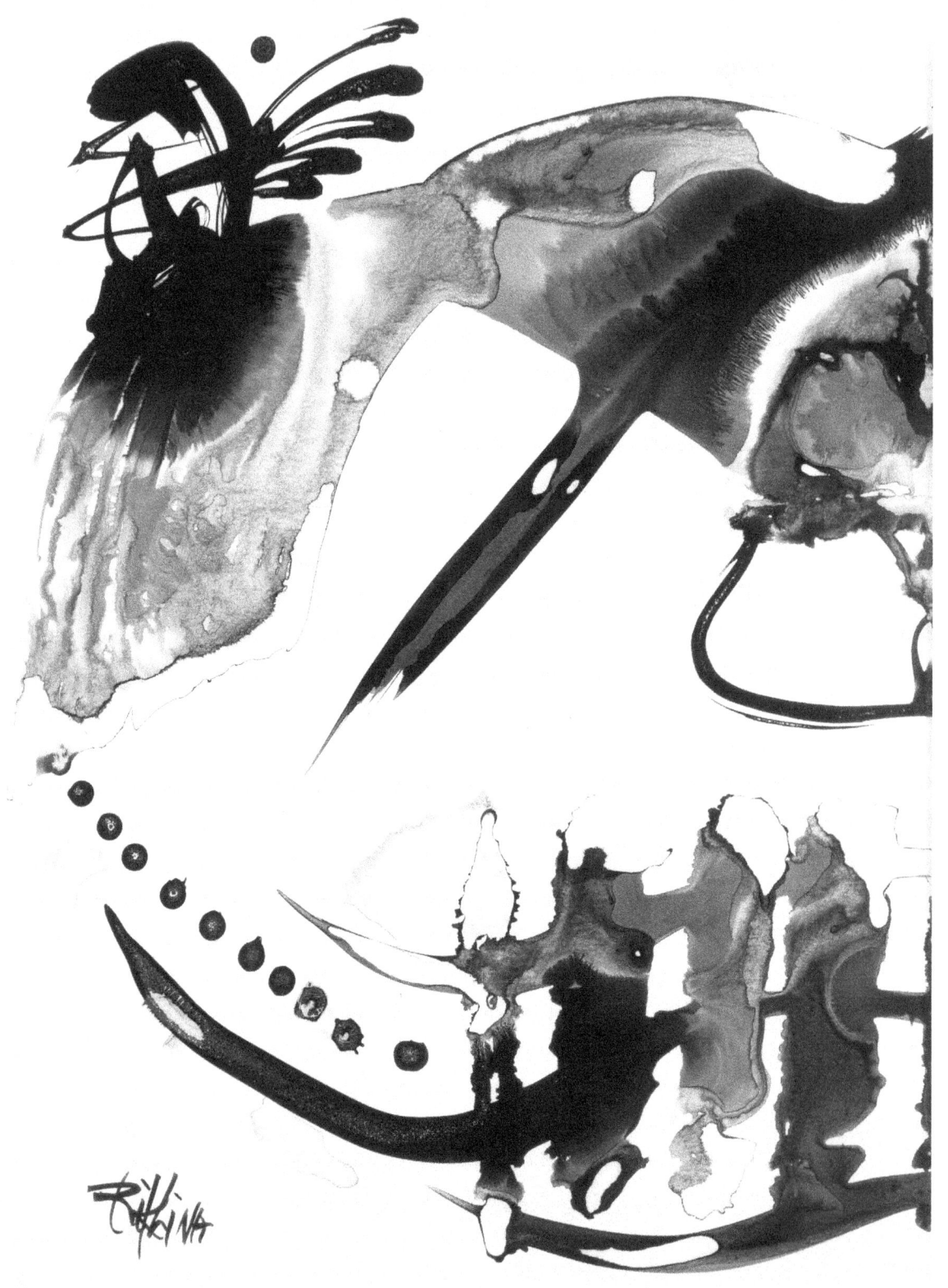

Perhaps
the serrated dagger
perhaps
the nude inferno lines

& we knew
that your body withdrew
that its self-suffering coalesced by paroxysm
breathing by general erosion

& so the fact of your postmortem occlusionary zeal
the weight you once carried
possessed ironic suns by short circuit & vapour
& the effects of your discomfort always shot out rays across
    salamander prairies

Again
neurology was understood
with its scarps
its possessives
its miseries
its bloodless ozonal effects
which burned by vitriolic aural report

Because your nerves so registered with the blind
it was as if mixing salt with general ocean water
camouflaged
as you peered at the human species from immaculate levels of
    the field
instantaneously foreshortening asymptotic distance

alive

with pure ulterior evolvement

far beyond the reptilian basalt

of hamlets & curfew

all the while you dug into soil

with shrillness

with sudden earthquake absentia

with broken & rebuilt fingers

with talons outsized

according to the scale of a Condor

Perhaps I can now describe you

as liquid impartibility

feed by waters from a nullifying spring

Or as an acidic flaw

or

an undocumented boulder

splintered in sets of 3

as if optically partaking in Giacomettiesque partition

This remains for me

diplopia by gerund

by a geometry of gerunds

so that language is summoned by aporia through circumstance

by assault which stutters at the brink of exhaustion

So for me

your ghost continues to flame

your optometry ripples through saving instinct

as you stride across the afterlife

by ostentatious liberty

by a pre-living ether

in what I perceive as the shock of your totalic embodiment

& your body at another pole of thinking

as ambulate de-incoherence

beyond mockery & scandal through interior preappearance

having knowledge by rambling antibody

thereby understanding

each opacious law as tornado

as ashen proclivity

towards depopulated postulate as utopia

Antonin

this is the equation you now explode

careening down a slope

towards a strange Phoenician ocean landing

where opiates transmute

where metamorphic inhibitors are understood

Thus the after-existence

like an amorphic compass

like a psychic canister holding molten as transparence

The sea in death being unchronicled slag

as a flowing curvature of osmosis

your body as it stands

being mordant flesh

being incandescent comet

The blaze Antonin the blaze

& this felt before death
in your trans-anarchic marrow
so as to hone and transgress the spirits within your spells
which turned apollonian mirrors into shards
striking at their source roots with tainted canonical tools
having more power than any one-seeing person

& so you struck out on journeys
calling forth interior flaws
announcing all along
your prophetic forthcoming
like thirst on a barge
or oleander pontoons

You advanced your own chimeras
which prevailed as clamorous foci

Therefore
you've never been accused of harnessing your spirit to repetitious
    safety
to a hounded prestidigitator's prism
with squarely cut glass from a conclave

Therefore I approach you obliquely
through fatigue & ground-down demons
with your seismically approachable dread
attempting to carve my shadows with a henbane scalpel

I'm seeing you in the mists with your glowering ptomaine persona
with your chronic angular ascent
with your transmissive gestures
having a scythe in your hand
like a snare
arrayed in the horrifying glint of arachnid's clothing

This remains your soil as drizzle
as ashen guttural ink
as violent & dismissive of albinos
not through blasphemous conservation
but by impact
as a European recreant
living under the auspices of your own distinct creation

I
who've had the strange insistence
of perfect maniacality as minus
all the while knowing that you knew the wastes of speech
through powers which invaded the grammar
not unlike a crystalline misnomer
or a tremor of light at the edge of a lisp

Because I am partially dissolved as regards fixation
I can see you hounding the scribes from your postmortem throne
    room
breaking up events
evincing scrambled logs & heinous cornucopias
with your hydrology condoning perpetual hesitations

& these hesitations being squalls
which tend to undo the harmonious surface
while being not unlike the mediumistic as ampersand
full of blackened grace & mystery

Of course
this is not a pointless hagiography
alive with poetry as seduction
sycophantic with structured myths
atomized & gathered with reverential glances

In your present phase
you are alive with great vigesimals
with burning wicks
with carnivorous stoking rums
& when I speak of you this way
I do not respond as liberty by entrapment
or squandered hail
or recessive thermo-sorcery by number

Yet the number which I reveal
remains the charged number
the insidious panopticon
simultaneous
with your odyssey as osmosis
over & above the skeletal as diacritics

You are not of the Passeriformes
or of boulders to be studied & bevelled & conceived by abstraction
therefore your body

not to be apportioned
nor misclaimed as categorical wheat
but understood as primeval dispossession
as if your body itself were reinhabited by phrasing

Thus in your case
ambulation by chant
by fabulous insularity
this being the inner scroll
Antonin
the mountainous inner schism
being blinding de-succession as sound

You being the lingerer in hovels
were ceremonious as de-invention
thereby seeing yourself
as iguanic by persona
by paralytic in-cessation
creating commotion by a density of drafts
underscored by force as fugacious telepathy

As if your body were brewed by omphalos
by mercury as circuitous wavelength

So depth & the body
were never summoned as weightlessness
as charioteer in transparency
always sitting upon a sigil as hypocritical stalagmite

No
you the worker in the tragic séance foundry

knowing in depth an occipital smell with its strange necrotic
    umber in motion

Thus a brutalized emboldening
your story as enjambed momentum
this being the mount of your shadowy siroccos
as entombed & erratically handled prefigurative
wavering as prekindled fragment

& what is prekindled prefigurative?

Acts of ecstasis?
unbounded gales?
sigils as posterns?

I now give to you
the crown of High Mongerer
flitting back & forth through morbid lingual data
as if haunting the crags across *das Sonnensystem*
& all the disequilibria
a rite
a curious kirilian disfigurement
hissing inside the occult
not as a de-invigoured leper
but as one whose odyssey precludes remorse
whose odyssey continues to invade by scorching conundrum &
    heresy

Having invaded my eyes with a baffling salvo of colours
for instance

orange rehidden within scarlet & saffron

then a blue/white exchange at the border of listening

where a double worm is hollowed out

by oblique subjugation

where all thinking projects its ferment

by precipitous despair

Can I say

an action on your behalf always transmuting the inclement as power

as depth

as data re-retrieved from confining in-solution?

Even in death this remains a micro-incisionary effort

over & contained isotropics as perception

thereby understanding

the body as shattered foundational ether

as prophetic incendiary kingdom

uttering within itself a maze of solstitial pronouns

This remains

Antonin

the body as evangelical absence

as the cry of a rural cheetah

or hissing ants

or sublingual remoras

Thus the deadliest self as somatic burial by ink

then helix as sorcerous bed lion

then bleak or intermittent dictation by foal

Again odd or subliminal vestige
perhaps furtive tablet
perhaps salt at interminate angles

So should one coalesce within an optic of fractious musical zeal
one could always re-elevate the cacophonous or tragic incendiary
    item

For instance a mosque side by side as two tables
the latter being blurred moons & scarlet mares
with a double harness lying beside a barbarous drinking stall

The above
a figment from a curious mise-en-scène
perhaps a sun which has been mislaid in a viperous old Albania
as in a scenario of threaded coffins
filled with luminous scribbling
with enkindled urging patterns
with your portrait then drawn as scandalous amoeba

Your portrait then protracted
as feral holography
as terminal drawstrings burning
certainly not a cauterized dilemma
but a feast which opens ghosts
as non-idolatrous photometry
much like watching herons fly from sterile onion trees

Such flight
not a forum condensed

by viewing or disposable linkage
but ophthalmology by percussives
by a squall of fuels igniting life veins in the eyes

In this regard
can I call you a thorn bird
or an opaque medusa suddenly forming in the air?

This is not to say
that you were created to circumvent a sudden hanging tree
or straighten an altar of foil
or manage an obliquitous stanza
there remains
your consort with the indefinite
with embrangled lakes
with powerful thought adjustment

This was your body as fuel
as enactment
stepping on stage as a wayward iguana
your motion which coalesced through a frenzy of blazes
through distorted election
at Hôpital de Ville-Évrard
within the despicable moats of Gaston Ferdière

& Lacan could never see you
as the incendiary greyhound
as the haunted schism overcoming its form
so you dispatched your thought in code
in alchemical bursts

in tornadic recitation

over & beyond the fabulous as iconography

akin to the sound of a stunning Flammarion dog

whistling

through blank mutative transport

Within such psychic concourse

the axiomatic is no longer mirrored

in strategized dictation

& so Antonin

I cannot linger in your presence

through sullied medical disclaimer

excusing my combat by carving bones in a broken monetary castle

excusing my long term dossier by partially hiding in a darkened
    aural forge

Yes

I live with a suppurating subtext

with a flash from exhausted turpentine ledgers

Again

there exists no ruminant animal excuses

no rampant grammatical insinuation

divested of pure adrenalin soil

attempting to study myself

through depressive incoherence

I am not excusing my personal solar yellows

nor gnats which glower from the depths of oppressive nitrogen fields

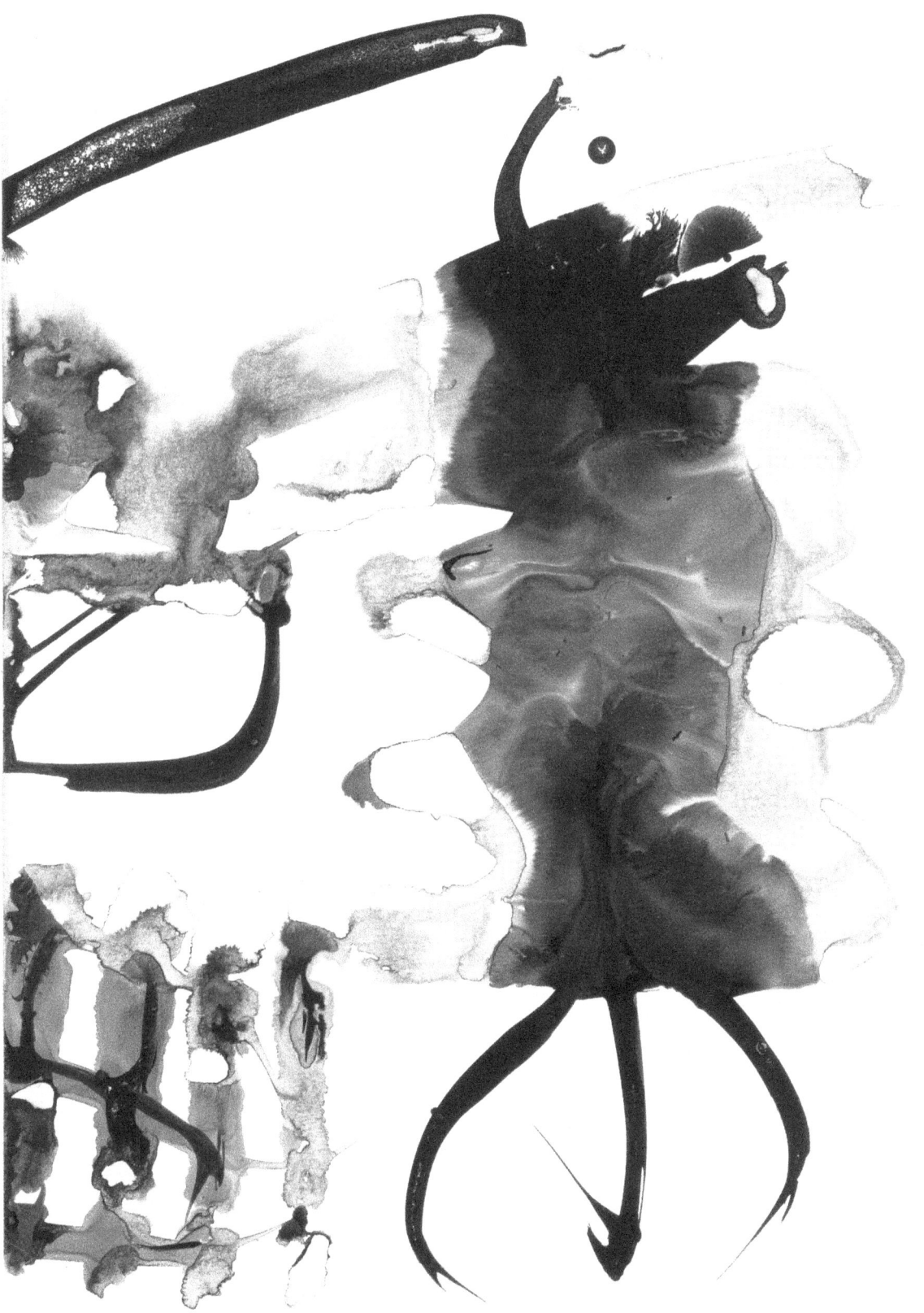

Although my teeth seem to be squared

my vertebrae listed as a bolt in a tolerable column

I understand your shattering

& all the internal weapons you accrued from your broken vertebrae
    after electroshock

I understand

your displaced interregnums

concerning powers that post-exist

re-erupting in your shadow life by double compounding

by a motion of shards & spells

consumed by proclivitous dipthong reversal

by compound cellular advance according to exhaustive in-conclusion

Antonin

this remains feral

remains an in-dominant lucidity

signaling itself by a floating remonstrance

& in life

your gestures continue to renew by oppositional flares

& each collage of recitation

has broken beyond abrasive cellular confinement

& these confinements you transmuted to tools

to dazed utopian byways

gleaned from your dimensionless gatherings

from your traitorous occultation

always colliding with the Sun

as though its light made provision for purposeless lingual infirmity

This was your body in life
which featured dark inscrutable thrusting points
an inferno of riddles
cast as result from reptilian mediation

So when derisives weltered up
you were not the person of the preplanned idea
with precise connectives rendered as patterns

Your drawings did no more than accrue mixed support
assuming in their odyssey a harried background of failure
yet you conveyed in their swarming lines
hellish thinking points
which featured a fugitive or thorny modello

I now see your body leaning against a pike
glaring from the fumes
of an onerous stygian window
which is not erasure or gulf catalogued as frenzy
as water in an inept moral cavern
yet the lines you drew were anti-colloidal
combined with blinding neural frenzy

As for heightening
as for the figure as perfect linear gouache
there remained for you
the Ground as punishing claw mark
as derisive umbra
as faded vulture's blood vividly scrawled as dastardly motif

I quote from the Greek
"graphein"
to draw
to define by insidious roundelay
so that repetition unminds the viewer
so I
as the viewer
ambling through an unstable mirror
understanding your element as insidious notoriety

& so Antonin I invade myself
as though stumbling by mixed pronunciation
by hematitic thought & mutation
not procession through indirected substance
but my eye as drawn by transluminal imagination
not as a moth
trapped in an unseen quarantine
but the bitterness of an egg broken & rebroken
according to the heat of a purely seasoned eye
rising from turbulent critical intensity

This remains the ozone that you carried
your ophthalmic ozone which has nurtured my eye
so that it dwells within perpetual turning

You depicted more than smells
you drew between zones like Italian Pentimento
through pure & naked graphite
through rapid distillation

Not for you the tailor's chalk
nor the smoke that casts its shadow by naïve aerial fugacity

Because I remind myself of all artistic method
concerning torture in white zinc
the Rhenish sigil
the flight which travels to a Tuscan infinity

The latter being the spell of the reverse of your shadow

Never bister or sepia
never the tone as wet or supple
applied to the figure as angelic moraine
because your visual enactments
remain as vapourized fixation
being light as shattered frottage
certainly not the image as opaque extension
but blemished dazzling
shifted across a kind of musical wood
marked by moving explosives

Can I call your pictures primeval sand bodies?
protozoic hurricanes?
the cellular premonition as eels?

Again
drainage accrued from imperial leprosy
from a magically darkened drinking vessel
being hive in disembodied nuclear form
as if you condoned this difference in Finnish laboratory rats
always linked by powerful tincture

Perhaps you made noise by worn clocks
by ruses which burned by decay
breathing prophecy of the unforeseen
uttering powerful reclamation of paradise

You spoke
of rotted fossils
of annoying beasts
of strange deflagrational organization

& by deflagrational skills
I'm thinking of the boulevard theatre
forcefully lit by disintegrated babble

Which is babble which fails to burn at your twisted saturational source
which was a source as a jagged hypogram spinning

So when you wrote on Balthus
you subsumed him in your text entitled "Facts Going Back To 1934"
he was "The Misery Painter" whom you invaded like a dye
attributing to Balthus
the grip of your old "obsessions"
attempting to rescue the painter from trauma
because this was rhetoric annealed to yourself
to your independent thought which hailed from disappearance

You attached personal antidote
to his personal attempt at suicide
through his unravelling over love

& his paintings
for you
an anonymous gestural hail
a form of occulted kinesis
inscripted by a precipitous viral tenor

As for Van Gogh
he declared your own agitations
he declared parallel to your own ellipsis the etiquette of self-debris
battling as he did against the world of constrictive social balance
against the powers which erupted from organized haunting
turned against all higher calling

You spoke of his "badly lighted" face which pursued you
which spoke to your essence through vibrational criticality
as if forged from a maze of cenozoic soils

This is how your shadow survived at critical peak
as volatile metabolics
emerging from the bottoms
by means of a burin encoded with an arsenal of spells
akin to a dorsal phytology
or a sagacious glossolalia of scarabs

& I can only state these matters
given that you wrote in simultaneous consciousness
as if on the one hand
ascending on plutonian stags
dazed to a certain degree by mystical ironics

Being a ghost in a gnomic dressing gown
you continue as charged cipher
as living vociferous monster
in the scope of present affairs

Certainly not a presence consumed by forms of Socratic farming
but a maelstrom house
a spiritual impetigo
against the pull of "time"
against the fort of "repetition"

In this regard you haunt the daylight & its rhythmos
with its mongers & its scribes
who etch the ledgers in Marseille

These are the beings you described
as cowardly
as shopkeepers
like worm riddled lava
like vicarious cows shot through with mange

So you arise & rearise from previous deconditioning
from a void that burns in your eye again & again
so you retain this elemental Richter
outside of life
outside the Sun & its schema
roaming the unconditional
roaming by instinct & its mercury
carving a path by continuous audition

which combines & re-combines
so as to shatter & re-shatter
gathering storms on other planes

When you lived on Earth
your voice was a protrusive onyx
was a fertile lizard gone feral
a categorical glottics conceived through furtive posture

A hibernating leopard
a compound margay
marked by spotted aural fumes
which scaled into view terrain as isolate damage

Your overall view was an exposed or ingeminate damage
over & above all collected terrains
inscribed by the history of monarchs
so your body became a hive of scales
which was coagulate as non rejoinder
because the body for you
was a boat with a body of lungfish bones
invisible
through which sound concurs as a sonic nether beast

So all feats of the mind became
like ejaculated scribble
as a rare or nervous sleep
subconsciously conversing with soot in dark volcano waters

This remains
as your right of indictment against nouns

always attacking wretched civil ganglia

for instance

the monomial condition of the typical tramcar rider

the imploded clerks

the palpitating bankers

These were the subjects you condemned

rife as they were with quotidian conniving

You struck sparks from a ledger containing a pot of gold & pearls

your dazed conceptions at one with Roger Blin

who worked inside your psychic soil

igniting the means of concrete termination

who understood your final judgement against God

as a "polyphony of screams"

"of assonant and obtuse rhythms"

"of insurgent elements of chance"

with your "black...apocalyptic laughter"

Certainly not a pre-existent dotage

but a clarity

a declaration

which overcame your poverty

your taunting insulin comas

You

who overheard

homogeneous neurology

the salt which implied an in-fructified collective

with its massless foundation

repeating over & over
its frayed reportage from culture
its neurons occluded
in a haze of self-colonization

Thus your sense of things
through a kind of vicarious alarm
yet all the while
bringing sound to a pitch
where the phonemes would boil
where imprecations were sculpted within the pyre of a stark
    inferno lion

Curses which you spawned as judgement
by curious & assaultive ampersands
with the power of defective neural scent
hurled against propaganda
known to the masses as progress
with its stylish motor works
with its corporate spinning jennies
aligned with the noun of tangible exchange
with repulsion after repulsion blessed by the ammonia of God

So how am I witness?
as interlocutor ?
as medial interpreter locating his posture?

How am I as the unknown scarab
the injudicious conflagrant
confident as alien transpositor?

I have come to my own amnesial telepathics
to my own inevitable volley of drafts
allowing imminent signals in the mind
as if I were to claim prime knowing of your struggles
of your molecules of fire
having first made notice of your symmetry
which always haunted me with contagion

A dialogue provoked by your works
provoking in me a need to clamber up the steps of your suicidal
    reason
which ignited in me the viciousness of study

This is how my signals project
when attempting to correlate with your genetic isolation
to the needles which struck the nerves in my skin
curing all hesitation in my pedigree

I
Antonin
feel privy to the insulin in your aura
to the buffeting it encourages
to the expositives it enables
expressed through unus-ambo
through the nervous sheath of a second body
burning
reflecting itself to itself
perhaps as a tiger
or a lemur
lifting itself from corroded states of wisdom

As of now I can say

that at certain times of day your body burns on a sand ghat

like cephalic reversal with all its specific contortion

like a blazing moat of spells

always moving back & forth as through botanical operatics

through insular waves of blazing nautical soil

shifting as a form of pre-labour

Your discourse:

strife

your modes & operations:

a stark incendiary rebus

I see you by means of the optic scent from my eyes

issuing noises from a stony electrical house

constructed in a yard

with the sky above its roof condensed by the indefinite

In my eye you've received your rain from the indefinite

so that its powers wash down with inalienable recognition

This nadir

this rain

continues to allow you range

through magnetic neural aggravation

like a hive of wasps

possessed by psycho-deflagrational struggle

& you remain in this suffering

as an in-palatable storm kite

which in your bodily life allowed you to focus on gouged drawings

on dilapidated crystal
on in-flotational barley & glass

Watching your eyes via Dreyer
through the magic of scattered aqua reels
allows me the feeling of being invaded by echoes
by charred transcendence
by apocalyptic exhaustion
spun by unknown gusts

Your eyes spun as if listening to music
as though you were predicting yourself before waking to another
 plane

So if I drew you in this era
my graphite would emit blurred noises
& break into a motif of scars
into epic conflagrations
harriedly conveying fluttering transcription
fusing your separate events
containing your chaos of surges
balancing your glow from furious anger
your image would then evince as power I would light in a grotto
through anathema sonnets
through penumbric whirlwind operas

& again
your eyes with their tense pejorative weight
casting spell after spell
through continuous combination

I call them pointed mirrors
percussive exactitude erupting as voltage

In order to promote results on this plane
you conjoined with secrets
which posted untallied outcomes
with your scorching disorder
held up by mercury & combat

By creating stark events
you camouflaged pure essence
by means of predacious scrutiny
opening the pores
to dense migrational unfoldment

All was infected

You held yourself aloof
devising yourself through improvisation & tremor

& this tremor has now distilled
& become a magnetic medicinal engagement
a desacralized contaminate
committed to the property of risk
riding in the altitudes of Mexico
throwing all your heroin behind
listening to your interior prosceniums
as a high venatic diamond

& you spoke from a level condoned through spontaneous command
when you lectured in Mexico concerning the "enormous error of
   Europe"

& its substance as "divided consciousness"
its energy "outmoded by facts"
breaking its empty diagrams
its bubonic explanation
concerning the draft of its own unhidden nightfall
& further
Marx & his dialectics "…an invention of Europe"
laced with fanatical commentary

For you Antonin
Mexico was not conduction by obstacle
but a feast which annealed the consciousness
with all of their utensils guided by the phantasmic
& I'm thinking of its living conduction points
the "Toltecs"
the "Aztecs"
the "Tarascans"
the "Otomis"
their utensils breathing by the art of higher lettering
by their blood as a silken metaforest

So for you
"drowned men" were poetically recorded
as was a "superimposed" rendering of "rocks"
as you so forcefully ignited in your *A Voyage to the Land of the
    Tarahumara*
"percolation"
dark ballistical advance
power as living alchemical shard

Believe me
I understand that gouache can be tonnage
that its hydra can be spawned by the facts of disinterest
understanding your sigils as unscripted manoeuvre
de-invaded hieroglyphs & patterns
understood by your codex as interior nucleation

I know by experience
that vicarious numbers subsume & indent
so I know
that their invisible compunction marked you
which starkly revisualized your original intent
by restructuring the scent of your striking nightmare leaven
so that your substance was publicly splintered
altered
as if your stark confabulatory storms had never existed
as if the crags in your mobility had suddenly disappeared &
    come to no good end

These were numbers without seeming visible realia
without ardour
or seeming purpose
yet always living with matchless initiatory fires
these are the numbers beyond labour
beyond backbreaking carbon
as movement in full ascent
as you confided to Riviére
that aloneness
 that blood which swelters outside of the cosmos

dwelling beyond visible compunction
beyond fetters which existed as undue mirage
beyond the effects of a single sun
beyond one's corpse as a single engulfment

I mean by engulfment
the body as living according to unaltered crystal
being above all false exteriority
phonetically heightened at each stage & all levels

You were born without the sheaf of intentional capability
with the riotous moans of a starving bear
wandering through blazeless polar invocation
all the while carrying a neutered passport into the galling world of
    labour

Thus you vocalized living as osmotic transification
not a crude or polarized continuum
but that which invaded the nerves like a spark of white vinegar
perhaps an inner humming which always drenched the atmosphere
helping you combat the boulevard with its writhing
your voice
a burst of artistic ravens
many times hidden within an ovicidal spectrum
alive with corresponding voids
through interior incantation

Because I have no need to take up on your behalf
there remains the simple fact of your unalterable circumstance
your mode akin to the sorcerer's depth

screeching through incurable magic arsenic as palabra

None of your actions amounted to prone or unjust figment
as Massieu in Dreyer's *Joan of Arc*
as Marat in Gance's *Napoleon*

This was energy unsealed
this was solar improbables projected

This was the transverse erupting as ether
all the while knowing
that I am inciting your apparition
through a seemingly blanched arcane
through a trenchant photometry as blaze

For me
you are both alive & dead responding through interior foment
being ruse which escapes the Sun
through phonomes compressed through a trebled marking action

Being apportioned by relentless calamity
you fought supreme approaches by demons
called "doubles" in the literature
& you named them
"Incarnation of Evil"
"Flat-Nosed Pliers"
"Those Born of Sweat"
they who invaded your mind
who stole your thoughts before you could think them
you being leper

who arose each day

from the depths of ferocious mental derangement

& as you

when I awake

through broken or greater waking

I glare at the map of my own cellular infirmity

never forgetting my inherited angularity

all the while surmounting the fumes from a carnivorous zodiac

with this difference

your mother & father wallowing in poisoned cousins' blood

where your despair was organically rooted

where you leaked your first blood from your soul

which then secured a life of gesticulating discomfort

Yet out of this chaos

you emerged

you arrived at Asia & butoh

at its oracular movement

co-created in yourself through extremes of inwardness

I'm thinking of an owl breaking beyond a hounds' cage

by means of great electrical yield

becoming in essence a spontaneous electrical spectre

You being this spectre

never monitored by jeopardy

by delimited source as instruction

but impact

over & beyond a cretinous scenery

possessing more energy than transferable coils

Certainly not simply a physical coil
posted in a windowless ground theatre
but being an owl with the Sun in its wings
flying through detours of accumulated psychic distrust

& you as this spectre
as this looming dorsal inferno
who arrived at drama through blazes
by alchemical knife points thrust into castles
like a grimace form through aquatic nightmare stages
so you were incapable of ruses
of artistic chaff
of de-invigoured contemplation

You who lurked
always writing a draft of intangibles
filtering your bottomless somas
with your body understood as tracing
as occult mirage
as ruthlessness through error

A nautical blazing if you will
a tsunamic unleashing
causing caustic pinnacles of light

Because your voice was a shadow in flames
a docetic cadenza
a hellish ballet

an excruciating substrate

but more to the point

I sense you as pure fragility by grasp

by sudden weight as invisible totality

You then leapt from this probing singularity

with your voice as a flashing zone

as hallucinatory core

as a treasonous mineral

being accusation through absence

A ubiquitous fuel of inverted burning

always attempting to undermine the compass of the residual demon body

so that its glints & parts of glints

began to spin in your presence

making itself known as fractious or cacophonous impairing

which groaned

which led to your experience by electroshock

which made your thoughts flee & fall skyward

rife with ill-begotten lettering

rife with suns from in-quiescent planes

You honed yourself to a peak

simply to speak with existence

to speak with its "rebarbative beasts"

to struggle with its monsters

your destiny being concerned with enormitive tides

with unsharpened crags

with fraught & foreclosed exhibit

So to renounce emboldened cartographical strife
to list with clear rhetoric
state conscripted psychic debris was never ingrained
your thinking rife as it was with rural omens
with seeming ossification
which you experienced in life as collapse after untold collapse
which was alterity pure & simple
with its bloodless gusts
with its cyanic nuclear wastes

Of course I am not here to take down your story
to create composed simulacra
to turn your passing encounters with Cécile Schramme or Jean Dequeker
into some enormous property
calling for some tempestuous review concerning basic principles of being

All your encounters were seen through vatic ambush crystal
always swallowed by the depth of your own personal engulfment

By understanding your fragile land body
I know it no longer partook of a European coding
the latter with its tense long standing cellular suppression
its brutish stones
its racial conquering epics

Thus you saw the Tarahumara and their land
as alive with a carnivorous electrical language
teeming with forms of rock struck from the cosmos itself

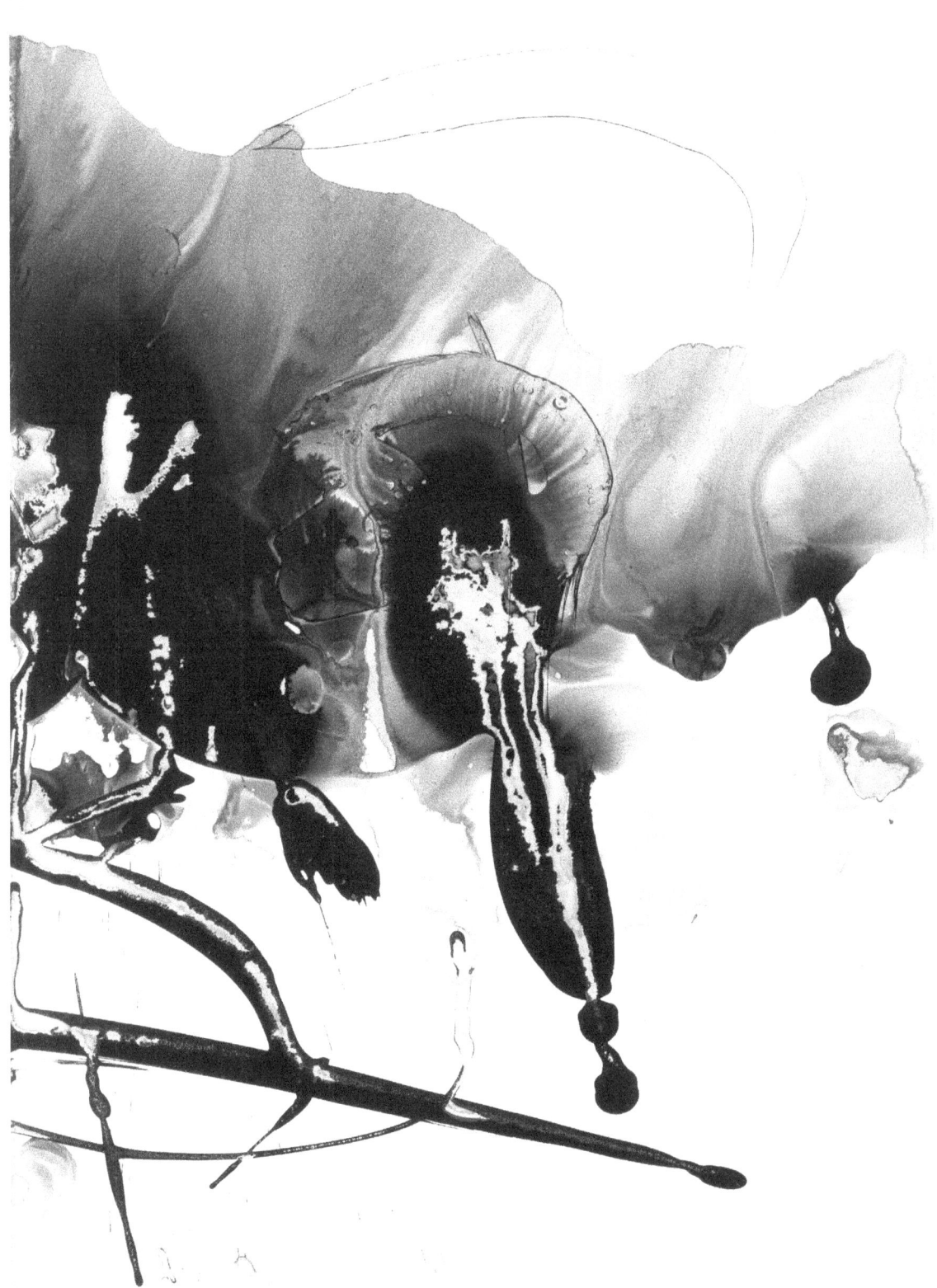

seeing its light as from a séance of flame
balanced between zero & its elusive conjuration out of nothingness
knowing as you knew the "unmanifest" & its boundless declaration
as crepuscular insufflation

Then you as I
essence centre plenum
"without body, shape, or consciousness"

That at a 2nd level
seeming mortality
as an injudicious androgyne
partaking of the "sacred hebdomad"
beyond dark or fomented incursion

Of course I've not scripted you
as divine coagulation
but as Antonin Artaud
as a fervent tangibility
only visible as a comet
elevated
fleeting
moving as heretical log map

Perhaps nothing of what I've written fully parallels your phobic
    de-ascension
your risk
your fabulous suture as leap
which transmits to me osmosis
by hidden gesticulation

Two questions Antonin:
how does one alight in manifest flame through feral & assaultive embrace?
how does one create true voyage in this life by the chronic multiples of despair?

& I'm thinking of your final embarkation
by its motion through chloral hydrate

I see in you a hydra with clauses
with blank motifs
with motivational kinematics
always erupting from your self of selves

In saying this I do not excuse my own distraction
concerning the charisma of your missives
or the power contained in your theoretical gradations
concerning theatre & its strife
& your last great words concerning the fiery cinema of the body

No
I am not Isidore Isou haranguing you in cafes
nor am I fatal simulacra of the ilk of the performer Nitsch & the Vienna Actionists
under the roof of a human carcass
juggling razor blades in the air
attempting projection of your life from a curious 5th magnitude

Within your pain there was a scattered "realm of bliss"
a "sovereignty" of omniscient symbolizing rhythms
alive with pre-eminent combustion

As of now I harbour a black or garnatic riddle in my mind
which breaks its own sustainment
which paradoxically creates clarity through magnetic fatigue

Again
I see you as a singular garnatic
riding on a burro up a mountain of dice
like a strange Indian in ascent
so unlike a glacial charioteer
with his guidance by fleece
telepathic with ruin

I'm thinking of you as lunar bell in the Mexican altitudes
facing eternity across the scope of the horizon
& I knew this
even before I spoke with the muralist Anguiano
who knew you in Mexico before I was born

The height
the electric trauma
your body keeling over from illness
all the while listening in your mind to the hum of Indian solar rattles

You
blemished shaman as fever
as energy through fluidic mesmerizing screens

For you
Mexico was "apotropaic"
was a contorted gazelle
not strategized by definition

or fact to be perused index by index
according to the dregs of a broken luminosity

Never in your odyssey had you seen such active regality
such cataleptic ascendance
non-engaged with facsimile or portion

For you
it was thunderbolt
tumultuous wraith
range of the spirit
opening inevitable solstice doors

A level of space floating beyond the fray
mixed with powerful & lengthy terminations

A singular living by indigenous plasma
as if keeping diamonds aloft as fragments from non being
making radiance out of woven blindness
as if
you had animated glyphs
from your raw inclement spittle

Yet
as you signal me from death
the doubts remain
the gulfs
the chasms
the tangled integers which you stuttered
as if you had endured yourself as a riddled concierge

forced to walk through deafening phantoms by means of falsely-lit
    effect

I could never call your reason
a terse or criminal fantasia
but simply call it a true implosional roaming
all the while rising through crossing & recrossing mis-supported
    planks

I know that you hear me
from a bleak & spiralling outpost
so that when I reach back
& call out the nomes of the Pharaohs
I will imply Byblos in Phoenicia
I will imply the soils of Arabia Felix
all the while rising above emptied mimosa canteens

Antonin Artaud:

A Glossary of Fumes

Rather than provide a glossary kinetic with biographical figments, I've chosen compressed prose because Artaud, though he is prolific with human contact throughout his years on Earth, provided us no ironclad grasp on the exterior dimension. Consumed by the charismatic grandeur of suffering, Artaud's taction with waking reality ignited his form of address to addressee as if consumed by the dialectics of nothingness. For him "Mundane relations…do not touch the kernel of the individual: the search for redemption undercuts all social solutions." His correspondents, as substantive as they were, transmute to gnostic foils within his swarming verbal barrages. Not that they are without their own powers, but they seem to have gravitated one way or another to Artaud's smouldering inner Sun, so there is never the one-to-one relation one finds in conventional correspondence. There is always the underlying realia where Artaud is "exhorting" or defending himself, as he himself once said, and I am paraphrasing, that the reason one writes or draws or acts is to get out of hell. Artaud's creations are suffused by this drama.

To know Artaud was to be instantly singed by his struggle. His correspondence, from Rivière to Breton, never resolves itself on the horizontal plane, or coruscates as day-to-day understanding. No one is left unmarked; one becomes engaged in telepathic endurance, for Artaud is relentless. There is no aspect of matter which is not engaged in his war against darkness.

Witness the fiends who roam the pages of *Heliogabalus*, or the palpable force directed towards the surrealists in his pointed accusation "In Total Darkness, or The Surrealist Bluff", or in his extorting Abel Gance to procure a role for himself in "The Fall of the House of Usher", or in rejecting Breton's offer to exhibit his works in The International Surrealist Exhibition in 1947. Artaud remains a free standing singularity.

For Artaud, the plunge into darkness was the overcoming of darkness. Simplicity of tenor was not a part of his character. Anaïs Nin once related that on a bright sunny Parisian day Artaud was exhorting passersby to overcome their inner darkness, which they clearly had no consciousness of. His warfare with the caliginous consumes all of his tragic moments. He is constantly hounded by the friction which imbues his body and his mind. For Artaud, the body and the mind were inextricable, and functioned as one. His fire was always struck on the hylic plane. He was lightning-struck petrifaction, unclassifiable, moody, plagued by seeming error, yet always staunch with perseverance. A perseverance which enabled Artaud in his pursuit of the Tarahumara, all the while engaged in mountain climbing on a burro while self-disengaging from heroin.

Unlike Cèsaire, Artaud's collaborations did not condone themselves in correcting the great social issues of the day. It seems he was always engaged in the overthrow of the false God whom the gnostics accused of holding all souls in universal entrapment. Thus he imparts his absence to others, so that, in a deeper sense, they no longer partake in their own biographical dimensions. Within this gnostic drama, Artaud's two dates of 1896 to 1948 become simply an ancillary item. His was the realm where only forces were exchanged. For Artaud, this was the true invisible grammar, the grammar where the superficial fact could never extend.

Biography as mere fact was loathsome to Artaud. And he meant by this, the author as personality. This being a subtext of his reasoning behind his rejection of Breton's invitation to him to participate in The International Surrealist Exhibition of 1947 referred to earlier. He states to Breton "I have my own idea of birth, of life, of death, of reality, and of destiny, and I do not allow any others imposed on me or even suggested to me for I do not participate in any of the general ideas through which I could have with any other man than myself." He states further that he has been "in open struggle every night and day with all the sects of all the sorcerers and initiates of the earth."

Artaud is not being subversive just to be subversive for his own ego's sake. He is uttering a language of mortal burning, like fumes from a broken radium fish. Radium, in this instance, not being a manufactured item, but of a cosmic ulterior order. As he again states to Breton, "The human body has enough suns, planets, rivers, volcanos, seas, tides, without still going to seek those of so-called exterior nature and others." Thus, to point up the gallery of personalities which hurtled in and out of Artaud's life would only secure for the text an impositional scholarship. In no way am I dissolving the irradiating power which issued from souls such as Paulhan, Gance, or Paule Thèvenin, or from the army of giants he made contact with during his lifetime which extended from Leiris to Vallejo. Artaud was a mortal striding in oneiric lock-step into the well of disappearance. For him, there was no colloquial stationing, there was only the harried rejoinder which sought to expel poison.

When discussing Artaud, when conveying his essential traces, all language needs to be distilled. In contradistinction to Cèsaire, there was no social extension, no concern with politics nor historic self-positioning. There was only the ruthless edict of personal liberty burning at the pitch of revelation. Trying to analyze Artaud is like trying to analyze the power of earthquakes or volcanos. Indeed, he was an environment unto himself, much like a sky beneath a flickering red dwarf, inclement, seismic, always feral, cataclysmic by means of its own anatomy.

                                                            Will Alexander

At the Vertigo Borders

"…Roger Gilbert-Lecomte breaks with the poets of the present day, to recover that organic note, that organically torn mood, that fetal, dank, fiery atmosphere that has been the hallmark of true poetry in every age, deriving its force 'from the life force and its source from the source of life.'"

– Antonin Artaud

Roger Gilbert-Lecomte

for Roger Gilbert-Lecomte

> *primal light flashes...*
> *flooding a living man*
> —Roger Gilbert-Lecomte

You as spectre
were trenchant proof
of sidereal inspiration
encyclopaedic with transgression

You as inscrutable scribe
who hailed from unlit suns within suns
as elevated omen
as intransigent cellular inferno
as none other than a flare

Your energy at inception ignited by ether
by higher intestinal order
with your stamina infused by furious vertical seas

Your fervour for the strange
for unclaimed & rapacious spirit
for a tapestry of various hellgrammites
based upon grammar inclement with dictation

Not a curse
nor a law spawned
nor a threatening hesitation fueled by personal convolution

Instead for you
a policy of blizzards
of spells conjured by vatic contagion
your cortex reversing the copious principle of constriction
as visitation from occlusion
alive with all manner of interior marking
singed by compressed phonation
by verbs from the beyond
by powers barely grasped
by the energy of elliptical hopscotch

& always you were rife
with indictment of the literal

You understood such attack
by means of raw philosophical posture
by momentum exclusive to cinders
which interacted with negation
with the crisis which contains itself within consensus embranglement

In such a setting
you knew all along
that consciousness ailed as a fugue of nonentity
as micro-annihilation
without having to any degree
a community of voltage

The populace at large
consumed as a fragmented herald
without invisible habitability
a world incapable of raised marrow

of Tibetan pre-simplicity
where the body is infused by breath conjoined by umbilical mantras

You experienced language
as a cleansed genetic rotation
spinning through the spirit as micro-amplification
listening at the plane of nths
at the highest registration of each phoneme
knowing each letter to be lit by hurricanes of trance
its background value spawned from a hallucinated district
the latter
a single portion of trans-cyclical glossolalia

& you Lecomte
always invaded by aural monsoons
you who surmounted sea walls at birth

& for you
never a garrison of bodies to be engaged
to be socially constricted on the quotidian threshing floor
always facing themselves in nervous mirrors
estranged from suggestion & magic
disengaged from the Egyptian electrical body
from its transpersonal foremast
never knowing the power convened by apprenticeship
conducted as it is in circuits of the psyche

Never for you
simply campaign as poltergeist
as social scorpion simply bent on attack

It's as if you engaged
sudden secondary waters
moving back & forth
across a looming spectral dimension
with never an iota of negligence
concerning the invisible & its accuracy
with its particles by inference
by intuitive shading
by imperceptible kinetics

Knowing metals to have erupted
you understood language as plainsong freed of all mass
knowing its motion as importation of drift
being insight by dopamine & dice
by departed locust mountains
so that the beyond howled with spells
with trenchant irradiation
so that you were never better or worse in your body
despite the jailings
the morphine
the indictments

At 14
roaming outside your body via carbon tetrachloride
along with "Daumal" "Mayrat" & "Vailland"
with all the exterior graphs sunken from view
all the railings to the void unlisted
all prior chronicles inept
as regards the body as emptied husk

as blank evaluation

as totemic inclemency

as to locatable transit

with you there was always guise through burning

through uncommon surfeit

through maniacal application

Rimbaud was not alone in braving the poetically unplumbed
before what could be called numeric maturity

You at 14

as editor-in-chief of *Apollo*★

your first poems emitted from the lycee at Reims

then Daumal

then the Simplistes

again the carbon tetrachloride

pure sidereal experience

your body as invisible lens

as unsettled munificence

as non accumulation

as draught of the purely visible

One could say that Roger Gilbert-Lecomte has gone missing
that the author under copyright is uncapturable existence
is never confined to telluric magnitude
never to be converted according to the poet as particle
who announces the family warren
through sentiment laced with its presence as shadow
instead
you rose up & expanded as dazzling refrangible chroma

As charismatic centipede
extending in all directions
as if you caught yourself casting shadows
all the while refining a true lenticular blindness
being a flare of heat rushing across enigmas
always getting the sense of juggled crime on random
    Thursday afternoons

For you Lecomte
outer law was never the dawn
the crepuscular presence
through which all fate was solved

You knew that pedestrian dossiers would be deleted
that all trace account
that all the harrowing figment of your morphine trail
would perfectly de-exist
that its zodiac would consume your biography as example

You Roger Gilbert-Lecomte
were perhaps a tree made purple by mirages
beneath a storm which rained as black suns
creating an aural fire
not unlike a field of wheat erupting from the brushes of Soutine

Vertiginous
wary
uncaring as regards extrinsic censure
all the while
speaking to yourself in dense galactic patchwork

A voice simultaneous with itself
telepathic with stratification
as if a bird had drawn its own blood & vanished
between atmospheric balance & sudden aspects of Uranus

Of course you were not sheltered from this balance
always facing the blunt formulas of life
mapping illusive clauses
across curious intervals of being
not unlike a cacophony of sand which concealed all waking ruin
knowing itself to be a voice which issued from bells
which rung between an intermittent lava

& I can only observe from my present seismics
your quaking pivot
your mural of privation
your blinding alphabetics
always testing your inevitable posture

You
Lecomte
the enigmatic puzzling ore
bereft of seeming inconsequence
by turbulence too concussive to conceptually recall

Synaptic shadows
which erupted by knowing the art of death
by knowing drafts of diacritical hyper waves
electric with transverse quanta

Thus the mind devouring itself
as broken navigator's signals
as verbal toponymy
working at differing rates as ciphers

Not unlike an insidious emptiness in the syllables
working on unnamed planes
part vertical
part draft as omega
through the human cellular locale

Human life
an exercise at cross purpose with itself
& each effort of the current era
seemingly ministered by an equivocal frontality
an entrapment
never ceasing to cling to a projected surface
to a militarised prakriti
as if all the gulfs in being had been annulled

I can only say you were an umbilical declaration
saturant with haunting
as a curious skeletal marquee
exhausting the realm of nouns
so that hidden possibility tends to exist as a draft
at the borders of a tenuous carbon persona

What the common perception would mistake
as an ailment of being

signalling itself from cracks in the mystery
attempting to perceive yourself as a compound unlettering

Because for me
the morphine was a sigil
an immense green buzzing
always covering your true ignition

Yours
as a wakefulness
far beyond the common sun
as helical power enacted in hiddenness
which for me
is a new ozonal form through language
neither *anglais* nor *francais*
but language as understood through drafts of pre-existence

You knew
as one exists before being born
its clauses
its struggles
before you surfaced as supposed evidence
in Reims
in France
in 1907
which for me
is not a numerical boundary
nor a placard
where there existed no previous existence

a period where recognition de-existed

where all was classified as a seminal non kinetic

I cannot inhabit such opacity via cognizant limitation

as if Jarry & Dr. Faustroll had never existed

had never sundered the molecules of "right thinking"

as with Rimbaud

who remains for me as enigma

who was able to enrich by fire

the verbal mathematics of canyons

knowing numbers to be the fire of pure air

You as haunted aboriginal millstone

curiously timed as magnetic drift

as organism sculpted by absence & burning

& it was in this condition

that you enthronged yourself in "the pact of the absolute"

with Daumal

& Meyrat

& the whole of the Simplistes *

playing Russian roulette with Meyrat at the trigger

giving yourself over to the plane we know as death

hoping to see in full force

the summoned source of inner suns

willfully cast from your body

ejected from its cage of fatigue

To suddenly explore the inclement

climbing atop an outrageous rostrum

as if squinting through sand

into a primeval testing point
with all its mirrors blown away
with all its muffling suddenly herded
beyond bodily jurisdiction

I call this state one of indigenous bravery
of blinding submission to extremity

According to skeptics you were deranged with 4 arms
with several teeth missing
like a wolf mistakenly entering a sand dune of lions
which I see as a sigil
which blossoms ancillary storms in my system
leaping containment by products & beliefs

Not a mimicry of the beyond
but true electrical immersion
being something other than academic consumption
not unlike the weight of moments
before the body conjoins with the infinite

Certainly something other than topological inertia
or a sample of foolish rectitude
which allowed you to cast rays through answerless dust
through abstracted insular safety

No
I am still feeling the flames from your anarchic shadow
from your powers
extended from a-retinal cyclonics

Such interior leaning
keeps me balanced between psychic beams & splinters
organically wafting beyond quotidian dossiers

Which is not an agenda journalistically wrought
sought by means of Aristotelian dissection
in this sense I understand
I am the whole frog swallowed by the cosmos

So as of now I seek not to delineate
rather I seek to blend with the invisible
with the forces which tend to consume us
by creating unbalance in the bodily arc

Lecomte
the learning quotient: bravery
unruly motion: gleaned from sending signals across peaks of
    shining mountain cinders
always reaching me
even though I were marooned on a house boat in Cambodia

Am I being obsequious
signalling you out for higher affirmation
secured in my motions by a thrilling seizure of praise
making little comment on the morphine which racked you
which stood you up in alleys
emitting a dense narcotica from your pores
avoiding jail term after jail term
until the barracks of jail seemed your second home?*

You with the trickery

with the laudanum coloured eyes

with all evidence leaning downward

falling towards Dante's innermost circles

towards his innermost torment

which in your case prevailed as an existential density

Where from time to time you struck the lightning bottoms

as prone unalterable abasement

with gulls mocking you from above

Lecomte

your language allows me to rove & listen

condensed as it is like a sutra of the uncanny

because I do not centre my audition upon the principle of carved
    systemics

I understand the strife

the squalor of damnable circumstance

which created dependency on Ruth Kronenburg & her seamstress's
    allotment*

seemingly subsumed by a polis turned dark

under the foul incessancy of Hitler

As I speak of you

there only exists duration

the gigantic instant

the simultaneous stream

the coalescing of seeming distance

Because all the while arrival happens at once

as if speaking of fumes
of detoxicated vibration
never knowing the power which burns as heads or tails

You concurred with Breton concerning verbal flow & imagination
as wine
as fire which ignites within the afterthought of the liminal
a telepathic ether
allowing "the pure dictation of the psyche's expression…"

Yet
for you & Renè
Breton was never the singular flame which illumined the
    "vertigo of souls"
who sought to place you in queue as a follower
as an in-dominate spheroid
who navigated the oneiric as underling
as sub-dominate ash
convulsed by summary rules & banter

For you always the river of the pauseless
of germination sculpting itself
as the raw art of silk
as the absolute conjunction of risk
where you said
"I who am wind from before all motion
Wind alive after the last life passes away"
wind which erupted from an explosive glacial port
wind as dialogical opposite of standardized coinage

Knowing its navigation to be
the distilled kinetics of a dark fallopian sun
not a functional quest
but rays as insistent foretelling
of how being inhabits figments
& of how they interact within the realms of the visible

Not merely the showcase of this world
but tumultuous interaction
sired within the principates of limbo

In this sense I cannot research you
nor examine the extrinsic figments of limbo
unlike the gaze of biography congealed as private literary value
I am electrified by the trans-personality
by its rise above the grammar of public terrain
with its desire for microscopic contradiction

You are not a hostage to be paraded on a fabled plesiosaur
in order to face conspiratorial elites
so as to populate the mind at large
with a one of a kind distraction

You are never to me
a disposable ointment
an anomalous crystal formed out of smoke
not unlike ignited graphite vibrating inside a mirror

You were an open nerve
tuned to quantum turbulence
always burning with being

Unlike the "West"
brackish with occlusiveness
with what the Indian mind would call *prakriti*
being broken energy scattered across the surface

You were never a clerk nested
inside property or security accounts
making up cranial lists so as to match
one official movement after another

You were registered by birth
by organic quarantine
not unlike an expendable amnesiac
feeding on enfeebled spiders
ensouling your life effort
as desire to implode
signing away seeming sanity by means of interior parchment
gaining glimpse of the "overwhelming"

The overwhelming
by turn
being torment
"exquisite"
"awe inspiring"
all your waking ozone
impacted
with particles
with flow from darkened solar flares
which filtered a beam of rays through your veins

& you predicted yourself
passed out on the street
rescued by Madame Firmat

Because years before this
you alerted us to this turning point
in your poem "Where the Prophet Stopped"
"And if…I happen to fall
Flat on my face in the road arms outstretched"
silenced at the bottom of your physical strength
this was your "night of bewilderment"
where you predicted
"And I will come back around you like the voices
Of great waters roaring under the vaulted night"

Here I address your oneiric physiology
your fevers which alighted from the invisible
& poured from your wings
a liquideous crystal ink

This being fundamental movement of the wayward
eschewing the public in its pursuit of oblivious pressures
not the contracted or the frozen aspiration
living under common assumption of monochromatic legislation

The general mind
always thrilled by dissension
by the parts of life
suffused by tragedy & omen
emitted from the safety of distance

Of course you were never the dutiful spirit
the boy child removed from the power of explosive baskets
instead these powers increased in you
as you excelled yourself
as a monger of risk
as a preacher of anagogics
able to square both sides of oblivion
drinking from its ether
immaculate distillation

Superficial agenda
can only list you as an enigmatic prognosticator
vile
obstreperous
toxic
inflamed
a psychic viper
a carnivore

An apprentice logician can ask with a smirk
how can one study medicine
& live off the earnings of a seamstress?*

Let us go back
to Sufist registration
of being collected at the vertical level
while being dispersed on the horizontal

The former as a kind of psychic pioneer
& then dispersed as a reprehensible remora

The presumptuous ideal
would have you cast in the role of Sumerian baker
decorous with intellectual abstraction
blazing across eternity
more akin to Guénon
concerned as he was with ancient tradition
& its living manifestation

Perhaps as scholar
as regional ambassador in a morgue of study
you would be considered
a more respectable pundit
a concrescent verbal engineer
wrought by sustained lucubration

More respected
for levitational experiment
for your powers which probed the perpetual
because to paraphrase Artaud
the infinite remains whatever date or era we ascribe to our moments

Thus we are all unnameables
boiling with salt
with lenses turned backward & forward
yet in the "West"
always panicked like gulls
like a falsely kindled jasmine

Lecomte
you usurped the finely honed framework

of the artist who suffers
reaping public acclaim
given honour for brazen vulnerability
but for you
the impalpable operative fused with obscurity
your knowledges poorly seen as uncanny drill bits
as a mirage of seizure squared by failure
never connected to vernacular thinking

This is nothing less than the republic of inversion
nothing less than demonstrative stasis in reverse
as if you were a plague laid at the feet of a statue at rest

This remains the common critical topography
not unlike the sewing of small stitches onto
the ontological portion

Rejected by Daumal*
it seemed you were lost
re-collapsing into seed
as a mammal incapable of reflection
or more specifically put
as an antelope traversing the prairie of the abyss

I am not of the comfort driven
awed by institutional genius
by the fixed effluvia from Dante
or Shakespeare
or Homer

I mean by the latter
study which consists of extrinsic parables
which consists of the already made

There is never esteem brewed from coded warfare
from barbarous consensus

Instead Lecomte
you were embroiled in the field of the occluded
in the non visible
in spates of irregular dissonance
never claiming for yourself experience of the partial
as in edited spates of a drawn-out memoir

Because there is this haze always cast about you
this haze of the morphine needle
& your socially disturbed charisma

Not even in death are you given the accolades
as compared to the dharma of Wölfli★
all of us knowing
his seismic triathlon in paint
his wizardry which stuns the retina by shadow
by the aroma of despair
by lightning condensed within fractions

I am thinking of you
as protracted elevation of absence
which spins & coheres as the tumultuous
as the blood sun which empties
& naturally coheres with the electrical as revolution

Not the cryptic celebration of nouns
stunted in old grammar
but of all obstruction filtered out of hearing

Because Lecomte very few can hear
very few can sense in themselves revelation by audition
or the transmuting of the habitual in one's being
the latter having risen from ubiquitous division of the self
your calling was true power by audition
being instinctive understanding as subversion

Some would ascribe to you
the verbalics of an inarticulate submix
channeled through remorseless congestion

For many in the West
poetry harbours a blue island sun
beaming down on postcolonial tropicalias
on unsubsided coastal rivieras
where the natives draw water & serve bread

You were not of the attitude of the White man★
aligned with exclusivity & assumption

Not unlike Artaud
you were summoned by a higher crystal
by an unnerving novae
& indeed if you seem cloistered
it was renegado by warren
by carnivorous substrate
by the loins of a tiger

Paris blazed in your era
with certain carnivores who spoke
with the aforenamed Artaud
with Breton
with the copious tenets of Breton

& I could go on with lists
headed by Gurdjieff
Péret
Bataille
with Césaire in his inception
condensed by scattered factional battles
yet you were always consumed by eternity
by summed geologies which mesmerized
which extracted the ladders from slow motion coffins
not unlike sidereal hurricanes on Saturn

Let me ask in general:
what then is a period of history?
what is a king or a leader?
what remains a vaunted circumstance?

I can only self-answer by saying:
failed treaties
the interminable as regicide
war kindled by non abatement

As a congealed Tibetan
I know you knew that the personal was not an asset
was not an overriding realia

The personality crumbles
the body withdraws as exhibit
& evolves to dust between planes
to shadows which faintly evoke corporeal explanation

You knew the harvest
which leaks beyond manifest simulacra
beyond shadowed registration
which opens out onto originating insight
where essences are maintained
where riddles are summoned
where the answerless sustains its own powers

Let me randomly quote 1927
"extraretinal vision" at René Maublanc's★
"medical school in Reims"
Le Grand Jeu cofounded with Daumal
then weekly meetings with Josef Šima★

A galaxy of art interwoven with the unexplored
brewed by the central nexus of justice
which in-scrutinizes all figments
all royal & intransigent elements
so that essences are sown
economies bewildered

As if all goals
all figments were bewildered
were brewed by purgatorial inclemency

& your energy anterior to 1907?

A proto lama circling in its wastes?
an exceptional barley burning atop a perfect sapphire pyre?
a blizzard made manifest the other side of the Milky Way?

These are realia spontaneously rendered
covertly non-planned
being energies which exalt themselves
as the eudaemonia of consciousness

If I were active with spells
I would return to the bodiless graces
to signals from Imhotep*
beyond the nervous regularity of the body as given

This being the seizure & release of expelled demons
of energies in a utopian sense
which will cease to plague the cosmos

Can one say Lecomte
that this is curvature of the besotted?
a rivalrous instigation miming itself by error?
that this is a maze which channels emptiness
by pontoons which drift through the in-dominate
through sudden holes in space
never subject to retraction?

This being absorption in greenness
in a sea of nitrogen & lightning
where minerals transmute according to the other

This remains the plane of cancellation
where there exists no marked exteriority
no intensity as craft
no chatter which expels & re-expels itself
as monitored registration

As you've said "Think
of how the flesh can crawl
In the night of the senses…my higher
Self may escape the lake of fire…"

This being for me
the internalized code
as alchemic guttural wiring
thus the body skillfully climbing a mismanaged staircase
magically traversing a perfidious esplanade
totally unlike an autocratic consumption
clinging to a backdrop of metals

Within this tenor
I am not baiting absence
or sculpting emulation
or atomizing my private tenets
to abase myself before your ghost in the beyond

I am simply a synapse coiled with abandonment
with torrents which lead onto nothingness
as if wandering through open structural gales
through randomly glimpsed penumbras

This being of overwhelming gain

as if Gilbert-Lecomte had never existed

& had only lived for his own thinking

as a sailor falling from a raft

into a teeming galactic compost

into a summary sea of photinos

all the while knowing in my sum

the true tremendum of yield

In this sense I combine with you

knowing true aerial vitrescence

knowing true microbial transparency

summoning a future of pure orchestral seismics

quivering as the organic lingual body

always transmuting above the unsustainable

marked as it is by an ulcerated apparition

by feral magnetics so that fury

& destruction mingle to such an extent

so that the archaeological explodes by kinetic erasure

This lingual body being something other

than nervous rapiers in a mirror

being the friction which surmounts its own thesis

& creates a technique akin to other suns

to other vibratory waters

being an immigrant of circles

into an organic alien neurology

into asymptotic parallels

where new dimensions begin burning
& become as non import
as regards the 3 dimensional ordeal

Thus one ascends to the impossible
to kinematic blankness
not of the labour of human form
always evident as organic mystical lava
non-contained by a neurological jury
always baffling itself with options

So since you've inhabited a body
we both concur about constraints
we've experienced as partial omnivores
as cobalt imposters
as annihilative raconteurs
always operative in secret
invisible in broad daylight
intent upon collective solar cure
intent on general rescue of light
by what the Kemetians called "coming forth by day"

This being the osmotic
with its roaming across all layering of suns
across all ammonias & winds
across all levels of hydroxyl

Not organic tampering with the sacred
predicting an eclipse by bad magic
or falsely deciphering strategic rills on Mars ★

or as strange deciphered chrononauts unveiling new worlds
by means of superimposed technique

But I prefer to speak as a rotating nimbus
always lighting the analogical
being an avalanche of spirals
"closer" to the "blaze"
roaming the mills of space
before & after death
linked by immortal conundrums

In the verbal body
we are not to be animals summed by garnatic blazes
linked by isolation & rage
their rookies gone dead in the wastes
which is not the same when I hallucinate & see Torma★
wandering through spirals of ice
all the while knowing that ghosts are of a secondary balance
incapable of power vis-à-vis the Ground state
the latter always beyond a brief or illusive scansion
not unlike a separable fort
flooded with unalterable illusion

This is where both our elements transpire
this is where we anneal without drowning
always at the dawn of the unutterable
this is where the poetic resides
this is where it gathers elements of birth
where eon crosses eon

kindled with buried forces
leaping from the zero field *
its suggestive regalia
"forever unfinished"
always alive with the sigil of blind change

This being language as pure frictive yield
ensconced as hesitation
never conjoined with the literal eye
to emitted ore transcendent with ferment

The alchemic always holds its force in arrears
at times partially appraised for its tenacity
but usually looked over & hidden

This being the hidden condition
the dictated wealth of occulted axial wings

The Ground
illusively expresses its condition through human electrical height
not through the bickering demands of inoperable judges' banter
which pontificates the literal
akin to journal entries & their apogees of suffocation
honed as they are by relational limit

Thus the heavens are diagnosed by asterisks
by a remote & disowned significance

& I ask in concert with you:
what is the point of such gainful embitterment?
what in the circumstance refuses to soar?

Perhaps a brochure crammed inside a cassowary's retina without
    hypnotics
without the crystallization of sunbirds
without the activity of valves breathing

For us to transmute through the wind of inner tumbling
to states outside the local solar locale

When I think of your planes of weaving
there exists the experience of the mystic's palpability
which draws language from me
being compensation for the string of perpetual penury
 always slaving
to gain small portions of bread

A trans luminosity being bravery on your part
never constrained by powers of prohibition
the ability on your part to plunge nerves first
into the eye of the unalterable
into the novae of the untouched
as protracted essential
as heresy alive & in command of the inferno

I find in you a particular ferment
always alive inside the dice of refraction
casting a summons no impact of prayer could provide

A free particle
suddenly appearing from realms
none of the conclaves can acknowledge

"Satan
a tailless wildebeest"
concurs in your orchards from time to time
allowing lice to burn over & beyond surcease
making them a nuisance even unto death
even in the throes of that which casts away bodies

Within the circle of pain you were the luminous *dopplegänger*
an infamous husk
a praeta with half of your maw on fire
a turbulence surrounding your soma
your phonetics emitted from this condition
always absenting itself from samsara

As for your life technique
it seemed always mingled with brackish aural sand

Allowing it to float on great verbal gurneys

These gurneys being
the conjurers
the barmaids
the "oriental" "Magician" at the "Algeria Tavern"
living alephs
"submolecular" topics
being motion which subsists
through dazzling "nonentity"

For me your shadows pour as interior grammes
being less than the weight of a moth

less than an entity of ciphers
in this degree you are an arc
as if you were shifting moons across a tree & its branches
like alchemic strabismus
as 3 grey/green moons
at times as a clarifying verdet
or perhaps a solemn sea on a solitary day
with a portion of this arcing provoking subconscious carnelian
like an array of telepathic washes
not unlike a general field evinced from the mind of Miró

Not that I am controlling the tides when I read you
igniting articulate conjecture between double abstractions
thereby eclipsing my mind with unsettled phantoms
reading the hieroglyphics of glints
somehow cast from a Bardo Lama

Because as Bardo Lama
you were between & between
knowing that life evolved as the body on Earth
always poignant with baronial deafness

In this sense you enacted the vampire
with his "nocturnal throat"
with his illusive "gravitations"
appearing between shafts of broken onyx lightning
suffering the "chaos" of the "unkempt"
hovering
always hovering

lured by flashes from exhilarated borders
from intangible vertigo borders
always cross-mixed with the interminable

This I know
you tended to row your body as a boat of unrest
as pejorative animation
as strife
as a grammar of perjury
as a source of demented ash

& am I seeing in this trajectory
procreative desperation?
carnivorous rot?
ancestral odour?

I do not seek to make of you
an alien charged by nucleic heavenly fur
all the while intact
shielded by a brazen cobra's venom
thus sculpting my interior assessment
as somewhere in between the hero come to Earth
to slay Roman legions
& one with antennae that always hears the absolute

An unfixed deity?
a scribe who channelled motionless motion?
creativity squared by the perfect complexification of dying?

It is the latter force I ascribe to you
struck by imperfection
as a dark sidereal form
as compound aeration
as complex fragmentary diamond
flecked with dialogical scabbing

The vernacular psyche would see in you
a kind of water gone bad
molecular imbalance
ebullient misplacement
claiming accursed victory over language
being a bell with contaminated spurs
as corrupted visceral condition

I feel in you this glossological dye
this contaminate property of uneven strength
which leaks
which entraps & unleashes fire

Lecomte
I cannot address you by engendered indifference
laddling ironic soup
in the throes of linear observation
or perhaps this is insight of a viper gone blind
possessed by all manner of evil

Thus the touch of error & pestilence
of maiming through consequence
having nothing to do with the popular spell of the moment

I cannot forgo blizzards
in order to assess perfectly wrought structures
or to forgo scandal & blizzards
to keep my mind artificially balanced
when engulfed by the beauty of inclemence

In this you confronted the West
knowing its brutality meted out in the Congo & Algeria
carrying its state of mind without internal future
without instinct for navigation of mazes

So you abandoned its hanging mechanical lanterns
its inverse gambling empowered by slavery & death
always seen through a soaked inferno of blood

& because of the way that you continue to exist
you can gain nothing from them
nothing from their official pundits
nothing from their extraneous assessment
always as they are
at odds with the ire of discomfort

& now that you've invaded my constant electrical state
you remain a monster from within
an apostle always threatening from the mists
from a strange Tibetan seafloor
with a thriving energy like a carnivorous pike
as if poised by feedings from the Bardo doctors
knowing yourself to be a soul at great risk

Not the soul which subsists in a porcelain topical body
incapable of hawks or winds
or Kemetic recitation of the afterlife

I can only state that you are not compost of the Pantocrater
privy to bad timing
to bereavement due to claustrophobic hydration

No
you were never summoned as journey
rationally compelled to speak
under a banner of bad rhetoric

Now I collect moons when I scramble the zodiac
which allows the composition of treason
an acid
boiled over into tonic
burning with dis-logistics
which resurrects as vapour
as neurological rhetoric
as spirit which ignites its own motion
through higher grammatical navigation
always poised to observe both paucity & submission
constrained as they are to collecting olives in a meadow

With you
there continues to exist great onyx fires
symptoms which risk themselves by means of gutted opium trees
being far in advance of the day-to-day as living

As if you were a messenger from Avignon

perched in a tense critical circle

casting your eyes up & down a ballast of doctrines

up & down their blank intestinal powers

knowing life to be condemned due to an allergy by grounding

Never confused as to the tapestry of your own psychic emission

perhaps savour from curious Slovakian quanta

always weaving the powder of light in your wings

rising daybreak after daybreak after daybreak

Being a ptomaine scholar

absorbing language at a baffling pitch

at tornadic remove

seeing through the lens of meteors

holding an unsteady ozone in their mirrors

& thus acuity emitted from spinning exo-medusas

from an untoward presence conjoined

with susurrant liminal phrasing

evincing levels above the pressure of mortality

vis-à-vis the culpable mind

You've helped nudge me into the nether reaches

ascending the Alps of consciousness

absorbing in myself the hyper dimensions

enacted within the Bardo state

invoked by indelible diving

with perfect procession thereby touching

the kinematic substrate as Ground

So by indelible diving

I am able to inhabit bottoms

a brightly coloured merganser

knowing perfect percussion when breaking the plane

Perhaps I am a miraculous Inca who swims inside sleep

making stunning dives

echolocative with voltage

as a phantom body swimming in a liqueous diamond lake

electric with quanta & pearls

Lecomte

you ignite in me this Inca of pearl

simultaneous as glancing ray

as enigmatic calligrapher

breathing the ether of clairvoyancy

creating from your spell an offspring of neon

capable of carrying none of its conditions

around the rim of terra firma

Forces never sprung from the skeletal womb

via diplomatic balance

retaining rays from an inferential Bardo

Because life with Ruth Kronenburg was cut short

we can only project the possibility

of the power of your personal offspring

Instead I always felt you listening to corpses

with their half-lit eyes

petrified in formation

This being my sensitivity

my whole regard for your phantom outcome

which could be dated & performed in the palpable

not that I am egregious in this regard

looking for certainty through conclusives

but ceasing to eschew possibility in all its inherent efflorescence

across your bouts of convalescence*

serving unclaimed time in Paris jails

conflict with Ruth's family over marriage

stark resistance to Breton

refusal of Gurdjieff through the auspices of Daumal*

alliance with Adamov & Artaud

perhaps a coarse quotidian synopsis of your accessible extrinsics

As contortionist

as primeval magneticist

there was also humour which leapt from your grain

As Simpliste

you dressed up as an owl*

creating in your wake

a doorknob of glass

a posterior hinge

who forged condensation on windows

your voice always humming in a clarion tunnel

as unbuffered menace

Attempting to scale your inherent molecular trapezium

going back to the days when you wandered the ruins of Reims

gazing for remains of occult symbols

along with Meyrat
& Vailland
& Daumal

You as Simplistes
far along the way
in advancing a stark critique of being
which raised burning in the consciousness
as strewn decibels
as vehicular intensity
always an explosive powder in your movements

As adolescent
you possessed "mania" for "escapes"
for "farce"
for "subversive prankery"

The Simplistes
advanced through powerful spectral waking
specific exercise
which enacted
"astral projection"
"telepathy"
"extraretinal vision"
"lucid dreaming"
"meeting in planned dreams"
"automatic writing"
& you Lecomte
"charismatic leader of the group"

In this sense you were offspring from mirrors
peerless
a charismatic noun always floating above parameters
of walled-in "physical" contingency
as if all of you seethed
as owls awash inside Tibetan healing stupas
as if the lot of you had gleaned yourselves from psychic registration

Away from terminal coding
from prohibitive notions of the other side
what I'll call great devastating tensions
cleared of refrangible obstruction
cleared as much as I can tell
of all blank & abstract bewitchment

Even with all of the aforementioned
you still cast a haze through my lens
swirling with various oneiric climates
viewing you across a riotous spectral density

Of course not view by means of craft
but energy flowing through the hum wires
through anterior voltaics
flowing back to the past opening to view

Your acute personal cartography
understanding as I do
your blank Tibetan humours
knowing the pitch at which your eclipses part

allowing me force through elevated contact
knowing your dazzling properties of instigation
its root causes
its marrow which crosses all manner of transition

Lecomte I honour in you the opaque
immense definitive motions of movement
not unlike a neutron star tumbling from a state of compunction
not in the sense of a lateral orography
nor a literal causeway compacted with codes & numbers

Yet as Simpliste
you ignited code & ritual by whole germinating stance
overwhelming spontaneous burden by the power of
your seeming disorder

In this sense physical germination cannot describe
or offer the substance
which debuts in itself as superficial pronoun

Instead I see you entering & re-entering various solar domains
as blasphemous mirage
as an entity no physical fire could light or withdraw

& so you remain
hovering
saturant with roaring
an environmental cadence
which sounds to the physical ear as a bell
with pure Tibetan underscoring
creating trances & spells in a cathedral of droplets

an energy unconcerned with the opposable brew
of conventional dialectics

As miraculous leper
you understood
as a kind of crystal
the pure mystique of absence
as unbound code across the parsecs
never humbled by reductive regional glass
or by pointless reactive effort
spinning across a gaze of static
yet you occulted yourself

The latter
being hail from sidereal Bohemias
vehement with perfectly kindled phonemes
each letter blazing as percussive concurrence
leaping embraced bullion
leaping a roof of ghosts
so that language alters
what I'll call Leonardian anatomy*
taking as proof
bodily diagrams from Tibet
always taking into account
"invisible forces"
"vibrations"
"wheels"
"currents"
all beyond the domain of the visible body

These being the stark coronal properties of pure contagion
which continues to populate travellers like myself
who open soils along the way
knowing your provocation concerning
the expendable body
serves at the level of a nervous inapplicable body

Subject to its highest gesture as an open mutational inferno

Knowing de-inhabited vehicular form
combined with the essence of self-confronting
always in recovery from synthetic error

Because the void possesses laws of living annihilation
you were able to experience drafts of primal flashing
knowing experiment through funicular tumbling
honing terror like a mason of the invisible
sculpting the non-traceable as amulet
enlivening spontaneous blessing through articulate vulnerability

This being the density of your second or incandescent body
uttered as diagram
as the initial stage of the afterlife
which craves its own subsistence through creative immolation

Its apparition spun in half
then subsumed in unspecified origin
with all of its variety evinced through private seepage
& this seepage we have no way of charting
as we would by micrometer an oceanic locust

So am I saying that I have analyzed surcease?

Or enhanced a lamp of invisible fever?

As if watching you escape a cliff of demons
by means of a symmetry othered by nothingness
& this nothingness
having nothing in common with Dante's circles
with their known chartings conveyed by the body of Virgil
hovering within the law of Christian decimation & fatigue

As if I could mirror your flight
across acres & acres of extrinsic mathematics
as if I could force a tunnel through an ozonal mirage
envisioning your apparition as a trenchant or corrosive fuel
then equating sullage as a protracted type of empire
as if the weight of history could compare with interminable revelation

Perhaps I am akin to a lama testing my utterances
in a vat of bottomless echoes
searching all the ethers for a magnetic global forest
a utopia spiralling with haunted eagles

& these ethers possessing the combinatory touch
of old Tibetan physicians
by one touch
gathering the bearings of death
or the chirality of health
as if the body wavers between these two indefinites
thriving on liminal portions
somehow above the constitutions

of bile & phlegm & wind★
the 3 markers of the human species
with you Lecomte
being of utter wind
residing in a Bardo summit of an unsummoned schist

All the while knowing the motions of blackened transparence
of all possible forms
carried in your language as telepathic alterity

Certainly not description
of a tragically formed countryside
but something other
something which exists at the depth of non event
something stirring without interval

From this dimension
I come back to a scene from your physical form
lecturing on Le Grand Jeu in Algeria★
perhaps you extended through speech
your instinctive inauguration of automatic writing
& your foreshadowing of Breton concerning this key inevitability
you being the perfect inhabitant of chance
leaving in your wake scrambled hydrogen tables
emitting "essential ambiguity"

Knowing in your writing
the health of the glimpse
the cult of the untutored
the nurturing of instability

You were *surréaliste* before the term was known
before Breton conveyed its oneirics to the world

You by then
a blazing sailor on a raft adrift
breathing by means of a dauntless incunabula
your compass always lit by dazed bearing
commanding plesiosaurs in your sleep through syllables
of platinum & timing
creating from your sound
the geometry of the unbeheld

Thus verbal percolation creating inner calligraphy as view
not unlike the Eskimo Nebula
with its "rarefied gas slamming into the cooler, denser gas"
"forming fingerlike features"
which form as "comet heads"
circling at primeval distance from its centre
certainly
not fixed
immobile
nor gainless

Which is akin to your energy my friend
which sailed beyond the collapse of your circulatory field
of what we know of Roger Gilbert-Lecomte
which has nothing to do
with the narrowed or decreasing energy
of biography as we've been forced to consume it

I can speak of your morphine accrual
of your "two major essays" on the painter Josef Šima★
your hospitalizations
your wooing of Breton
your changing of name
your support of Aragon against charges of sedition

Your joining with Breton & Crevel
the "Association of Revolutionary Artists & Writers" ★
your break with Daumal
your slow motion suicide at Madame Firmat's ★

Some would call you
a blind cannibal searching amidst cobras
urged on by fever
encoded with subconscious blizzards
all the while living on planes of tornadic auroras
scattered across galaxies
across chaos inferred by non-human motion
at speeds which transcend the length
between the Earth & the Moon
moment by unparalleled moment

The exploratory powers alive in your DNA
akin to reckless lemmings
shifting between "sand" & the "fires of hell"
imbibing bowls of "undrinkable brine"
sailing beneath the dead
"…to earth's central inner peak…"

Lecomte
I think of the 100 billion galaxies
so far visually sighted
so I cannot think in terms of limit
of the anthropomorphics inlaid by the Christians
implanting the notion of one life & one death
on this planet
under a minor eschewable Sun
as if a billion galaxies possessed
an absence of genetic hydroyxyl
having known in your struggles "the agony of the universe"

Again
not restricted to this agony
with its bony chariots entangled in dread
by constructed explanation
constrained at one level as furious chatter
& at another
more as shamanic domain
the speech of blind silence at the centre of things
where only the inscrutable adheres
where what appears to be God is simply another cavern
another force within itself
only lasting until another universe appears
minus sustained calcification

You ignite in me such a survey
such a weddedness if you will
to all the suns implied by the alphabet that is the genes

An instinct
a simultaneity
as power prior to light itself
instarring in your vortical mirror
the infinite & what it beholds in this region after the Earth has
    disappeared

In this I see your dust of genius
your irradiated personal ore
being in your case the phantom irradiation of language

Certainly not a fiendish moral celebration
but always understanding your feats of pure wildness
your arcane sarcastics spewing from your system
as an in-judgemental recluse
at the cusp of disappearance

You as ray with eclipse light sensitivity
being an inverse sun rising inside a recluse body

& I mention the recluse body
as a migrating pulsation across the mirror of death
not as some wave of salvation
transmitted by exteriorized portion or particle
but by a base array of miracles
risen above distraction

& these distractions teeming
inside the damned & within
the lodgings of the not quite damned

This is why you have remained amongst the missing
amongst the squail of the dis-recognized
as alien provocateur
only partially explored like the Rio Alseseca★
rising from an unknown source
while flowing to an unknown source

& I classify your actions
as a presence of spontaneous sigils:

1937: "arrested for dealing drugs"; possible visit to Ireland

1939: living on "Rue de Canettes; near Saint-Germain-des-Prés"; arrested twice for dealing

1940: "refusal to heed Adamov by making exit to the unoccupied zone" of France

1942: Ruth Kronenberg captured; collaboration with Adamov: a series on the German Romantics in *Comœdia*; "Vacancy in Glass" appears in *Revue française*; NRF publishes your review of Jouhandeau

The above being portion
as mixture
as uncapturable delineation
as inflamed persona breathing the dialectics of crime

Perhaps a cycle of blind alleys
partially ascribing to your presence
a fixed topical a-rhythmic

Applying to your motion random visual expertise
an erratic line ensues
which erupts from perpetual brokenness
an apparition in an unsettled vacuum

An incandescent roulette
unmoored
in broken umbilical clothing

Nothing was bound to you
life being a raffish immersion in enigma
your endeavours late in life
always took root in the graceless
swirling with hawks & self-throttling

In contradistinction to this
writing became for you
the fatigue of lingual connections
"that instability of the soul"
instilling in your expression
the anomalous blaze
the uncanny
the auric vertigo of behaviourial conflagration
carrying in its wake behaviourial subatomics
a bottomlessness
neither attached nor conjoined
always crossing substance with its source in the unseen

Unlike Daumal
you considered no transition

between visibility & its counterpart
the incremental
the interstitial crossing between the two
possessing an absence of grammar in your outlook
instead for you
there was literal flight into heightening
you being the beak of the eagle kinetic at the border of empyreans

Not that I find fault
nor approach you with wavering in my system
entangled by imbibing second thought
I am with you in the overthrow of chronic tapering of the mind
with its aborted forces
its institutional chiseling
its Greco-Roman amperage

& this amperage at best
is a fundamental leakage
staining itself with a brusque voracious iodine
attempting to reinhabit itself by means of strictured tornadoes
thereby opening the poison of a simulated beckoning
yet always occluded by a precarious optical hydrogen

You as pioneer of the perpendicular
taking on decimation through oneiric risk
breathing the dialogistical as alphabetic unison

Like Daumal
you had evolved the paraoptic as epidermal depth chart*
able to distinguish differing hues

the jackets of books
from the fumes of touch
thereby seeing written script sealed in bolted drawers

According to Meyrat*
a dangerous period indeed
where the body became defined by vertigo at its optimum
being trance which inhaled the wayward
which opened itself to torrential expanse
not unlike thinking
through cellular hieroglyphics
on a plane unencumbered by extrinsic ideologies

When Breton configured
that you carried the aura of one that had been left behind
I fail to register his old assessment
existing as he was in the fatigue of curious circumstance*
what with the expulsion of Trotsky
& the general state of Stalinist error & its aftermath

This being the concussive dossier
from which Breton expounded at the Bar du Château
& you with Daumal
invoking by your presence
the anti-contingent risen
above the weight of Communist refraction
replete as it was with ominous social commandment
knowing as you knew that you had opened
a torrential criticas of the unseen

You existed by means of breath of this yoga
as bodiless sidereal zodiac
in keeping with suns alchemically leached from visibility

You
technician of the "essential"
a magnet floating at the edges of mists

Not as some mystic electrification
responsible for acolytes
confusion & gossip
for followers who reeked from attempt at the transformative
seeking for your response as all knowing
thereby creating in you claustrophobia by personal drain
not unlike Hazrat
emptied by constant questioning & demand

As if the higher states could be ordered by personal legislation
by extrinsic class grouping
weighed on a scale of metal
to be ingested & realigned
by a group of awkward Europeans

The latter emerging from gross monarchial saunas

On the other hand
you predisposed to damnation
plunged into episodes replete with non arrangement
only open to the voice which leapt into itself
as perfect fire of the arcane

always scribbled in the margins
of garrulous beauty & wisdom
of the penetrant sound of an unceasing river
through "toxicomania"

You
being the great asterisk
the immaculate saboteur
manifest through substates
through toxic incidentals
through anarchic multiple imparting
always casting solar storm from your eyes

You
essence of Le Grand Jeu
as fragment or ghost
escaping from extinguished stars
suffused with a light not unlike the colour of a harvest moon

An orange & red enigma
whom outshone all forms of non-conscripted chance
perhaps a line of lava as a moebius loop
simultaneous & surrounding with an energy far beyond
the dictation of "rats"

"Submolecular" as "ether"
as "crystal" fountain
as "wonderous emptiness"
unclaimed by brass or stitches
or from a mirror of dual or inert brightening

You seemed to learn from yourself
skills which formed from an astral summons
crossing over & back from death
as invisible aurora
enkindling speech
as a transverse tumbling
by innumerable windings
as fed on powerful sleepeater's rye

Yet you "who could peel the mask off your face"
& the "opaque" nature of the "skin's" "frontier"
thereby could reach the "fulcrum of the self"

This remained for you the highest ray in life
always challenging the corporeal
with its carnivorous quest for tactility & capital
witness *Le Grand Jeu* as journal & the paternalistic
quorum it garnered from *Mercure de France*★

This within the brusqueness of an atmosphere
rife with guilt of the general exploiters
ceaselessly clinging to foregone symbols
mired as they were in your dark inescapable eyes
subverting their eyes so much so
that no eye could see you

You were the one intrepid figment
never casting from your torment
the lisp of collapsed auras
or a displayed body stumbling over rocks

In this sense I am thinking of your astral comportment
of the telepathic Lecomte
of the oneiric Lecomte
all of the above synonymous
with the haunted raconteur

A spectacular biocognition
condoned by the flames of philosophical charisma

I think of your essay
"The Force of Renouncements" *
its coded energy which stemmed from abstention
which engaged the body as meditative husk
as purge of common creatural comforts

Not that I am surmising
but I'm saying this from my view
through extra-sensitive balance
which floats through shadows
which reaffirm your leanings
testing my own proto current
not limited to conjecture
but by intuitive intermittence
not having *Le Grand Gallimard* at hand

I parenthetically turn
to a trenchant note on Sanskrit
every "letter"
a "seed syllable" which manifests "pure energy"
being "sound as direct derivation"

not witticism crafted in opaque albino
galvanized to pointless personal method
to microscopic habitat
so that the great concussive storms are dismissed
so that the great zodiacal chartings are left blank

Let me quote Daumal on interior verbal irradiation
which supercedes "perpetual" opacity
by means of errorless quoting
glossaries of ether
through scriptural incandescence

Thus the voice invaded by signs of "interior research"
being self-collaboration which surmounts obscurity
being something other than a transitory spiral

It being essence as animation
"shining…its own evidence"

For iconoclasts chained to the visible
these remain stark inscrutable regions
without borders of balance or conquest
with personality cast aside
as dross
as pointless portion
as suffocating prakriti

Lecomte
without a guide in this regard
you were not unlike Artaud

spun in a zone
between personality & its absence
between one's birth name & quintessential gnosis

Lecomte
your mastery was the 2nd wind
that wind blowing from mysterious astral alchemics
that wind
which the Bardo Lama knew as essential guide
non-measurable
without aperture according to colour
according to properties spelled out as geographic facets

Thus the geographical as ballast
as known binding
as empirical coherence

So language in this sense
is neither "object"
nor imposed "emotion"
but the confirmation of phonemes through feeling
sub-subsuming in their wake transitory pablum
all the while listening to themselves as a choir of gold

The latter being
constant susurration flowing through the nerves
which congregate
as "aptitude"
as "internal conformation"
as prowess through great technical height

being exercise which spans the cosmos
all of the above remained your criteria for language
remained your roots in the unseen
in the Indo-Tibetan lighted by a darkened juniper Sun

Certainly not the temperament of Northern reasoning
with its harbouring of distraction
with its collective dossiers always tipped towards the extrinsic

There was never the superficial about you
the falsely-lit palace with its superimposed aurum
stenciled on paper as literary status
as inferior fuel
replete with pointless judgement

You have emerged in this era
as a field
not limited as spectre
nor as energy doubled up as in a withdrawn blizzard

No
you were never the corpse of immobile letters
drawn to scale as an old French bodice
in-circular
congealed by posthumous rhetoric

Due to populist conscription
you remain a darker element
mired in a cusp of seeming secondary yield
where subsequent rays & bodies of rays
emerge as indefinite syllables

Perhaps you are sending us codes from the cyclonic state
from its eruptive borders
where the cells exist as shadow
being inchoate contagion
as percolating cusp
as both inner & outer
as simultaneity
as curious tenuousness
where not even phantoms can cohere

This being the depths of the moebius plane
where a dark vehicular opiate exists
being both stellar
& personally trans stellar
at the vertigo borders
where the Sun fades in & out of motion
where the genetic cusp
begins spreading across unknown directions of the cosmos
where one can never predict
the size or form of apparitions
according to scripted scales of registration

As I row across your aural seas
inside your hyphenated gasps
which in the deepest sense are intervals
are shores inside shores
are spontaneous engulfments
which enriches me
by knowing glycerin bodies

post-carbon inscriptions
which in turn provoke the unbelievable

I'm thinking of forms where no history has invaded
no Visigoths
no Huns
no shadowed saviours
as if partaking of a power
the far side of an emptied body
where human script remains dissolved

This being the ray you invigoured
a zone Hamlet abstractly broached
throughout his protracted monologue

I call this the sidereal psyche
where human conscription
departs ways with itself

There remains the indefinite
with transition across impulsive extremity
which dissipates
& turns into a gulf tornadic with mirrors

Glossary for At the Vertigo Borders

<u>Apollo</u>—Ephemeral magazine founded around 1921 by Lecomte, of which he was editor-in-chief, along with René Daumal, Robert Meyrat, and Roger Vailland. At the time Lecomte and the others were in the equivalent of the eleventh grade.
p. 88

<u>Simplistes</u> (or *Les Phéres Simplistes*)—"A name derived from the spelling technique of their heroes," including the earliest Absurdist, Alfred Jarry. They (Lecomte, Daumal, Meyrat, Vailland) sought "to attain the intuitive and spontaneous simplicity of childhood."
p. 94

<u>until the barracks of jail seemed your second home</u>—Lecomte was arrested many times due to his issue with drugs. He spent his entire "inheritance on drugs…"
p. 96

<u>& live off the earnings of a seamstress</u>—The seamstress Ruth Kronenberg supported Lecomte between 1935-1937 with her earnings. They lived "on the outskirts of Paris, on the Rue Friant."
p. 103

<u>Rejected by Daumal</u>—René Daumal broke off his friendship with Lecomte in 1934. As Daumal stated, "the relationship was broken off by me when I at last saw that its hidden objective and visible results were to mutually justify us in our respective weaknesses, to exempt each of his responsibilities in the other's eyes…"
p. 105

(Adolph) <u>Wölfli</u>—A visionary painter institutionalized for life in Switzerland where he created his astonishing works.
p. 106

<u>You were not of the attitude of the White man</u>—Lecomte early on had turned his back on the gift of privilege. The Simplistes and Le Grand Jeu were naturally anti-colonialist from the outstart. Daumal stated that both he and Lecomte were suffused with the risk of life and death on a concrete non-theoretical level, and were threatened by the same forces that inflicted mayhem on the indigenous world.
p. 107

René Maublanc—These were the days of great experiment and personal risk. The year was 1927. The same year that Le Grand Jeu, which in English means "The Great Game", was founded. Roger Vailland had proposed the name. René Maublanc was a professor and fellow spirit who lent his abode for extraretinal experiment, and for other forays, such as out-of-body experience. p. 109

(Joseph) Šima—Czech painter. Regular contributor to the journal *Le Grand Jeu*, and, starting in 1929, served as the journal's artistic director. Šima was a friend not only of Lecomte, but also of Daumal and Vailland. He illustrated many of Lecomte's works. p. 109

Imhotep—Aboriginal polymath. Imhotep served under King Djoser during the Egyptian Third Dynasty; he was the "earliest known architect," engineer and physician. p. 110

or falsely deciphering strategic rills on Mars—I'm thinking in this context of secretive space technology concerned with falsely covering the active land life on Mars. p. 114

(Julian) Torma—"Due to his elusive behaviour and the impossibility to check his life facts...having long died before the publication of his books, no professional career, no fixed address, his body having never been recovered," it has been suggested by some, including Jean-François Jeandillou, that Torma's existence may be fictitious. p. 115

leaping from the zero field—Not as empty space, but as the ground state, the lowest energy state of a particular field. p. 116

across your bouts of convalescence—During 1930 "Lecomte is hospitalized in clinics for withdrawal from drugs several times" through the course of the year. p. 127

refusal of Gurdjieff through auspices of Daumal—During 1931 "Daumal moves towards Gurdjieff: he tries unsuccessfully to convert fellow members of Le Grand Jeu group, including Lecomte." p. 127

you dressed up as an owl—During the early days of the Simplistes, Daumal, Lecomte and the group were prone to pulling off intensive pranks, while at the same time maintaining a very high level of academic excellence. p. 127

That I'll call Leonardian anatomy—The visible 3 dimensional anatomy. p. 131

<u>of bile & phlegm & wind</u>—The three principle humors in Tibetan medicine.
p. 134

<u>lecturing on Le Grand Jeu in Algeria</u>—In March 1928 the first issue of *Le Grand Jeu* comes out; Lecomte changes his name to Gilbert-Lecomte, and gives a lecture on Le Grand Jeu in Algeria.
p. 134

<u>your "two major essays" on the painter Josef Šima</u>—Both essays were written in 1926. Šima was a "life-long influence and friend" of Lecomte. By the end of 1928 Lecomte is "addicted to opium."
p. 137

<u>the "Association of Revolutionary Artists and Writers"</u>—During this period Le Grand Jeu "goes into final crises." Lecomte comes out of his "opiate addiction", and completes by August "most of the poems" in *La Vie l'Amour la Mort le Vide et le Vent (Life, Love, Death, the Void and the Wind)*. He joins along with Breton and Crevel the Association of Revolutionary Artists and Writers. It was a turn towards the outside world.
p. 137

<u>your slow motion suicide at Madame Firmat's</u>—Madam Firmat found Lecomte unconscious on the street in Nazi-occupied Paris. She takes him in and he spends the rest of his life in the backroom of her establishment. When he died on the last day of 1943 at 5:45 in the afternoon, Lecomte had spent the greater part of four years at Madame Firmat's.
p. 137

<u>only partially explored like the Rio Alseseca</u>—A short interior river in Mexico that comes from "dormant volcano La Malinche." It is a treacherous river located in Puebla, Mexico.
p. 140

<u>you had evolved the paraoptic as epidermal depth chart</u>—This refers to the extra-retinal experiments of the 1920's in which colors were perceived without normal optical means.
p. 142

<u>According to Meyrat</u>—In the late 1970's Robert Meyrat stated that during the period of the late 1920's the Grand Jeu group was engaged in astral travel wherein they left their bodies behind and made "extradimensional contact."
p. 143

<u>existing as he was in the fatigue of curious circumstance</u>—The year is 1930. Lecomte and Daumal are wooed by Breton to join the surrealists; they both decline the invitation. Breton and the surrealists are clearly at a crossroads where exterior commitment and the interior world intersect.

This was the time when Stalin expelled Trotsky from the Communist Party for the latter's struggle against bureaucracy. It was a period of great strain for Breton. p. 143

<u>quorum it garnered from Mercure de France</u>—A French gazette and literary magazine first published in the 17th century, *Mercure de France* evolved into becoming a publishing house; it was never affiliated with *Editions Gallimard*. They originally agreed to publish *Le Grand Jeu* 4 which was dedicated to "experimental metaphysics." The issue did not appear until 1977 when the complete set of *Le Grand Jeu* was reunited and printed. p. 147

<u>"The Force of Renouncements"</u>—Lecomte's essay which was published in 1928 in the premier issue of *Le Grand Jeu*. The text was influenced by Hindu theories of non-duality and renunciation. p. 148

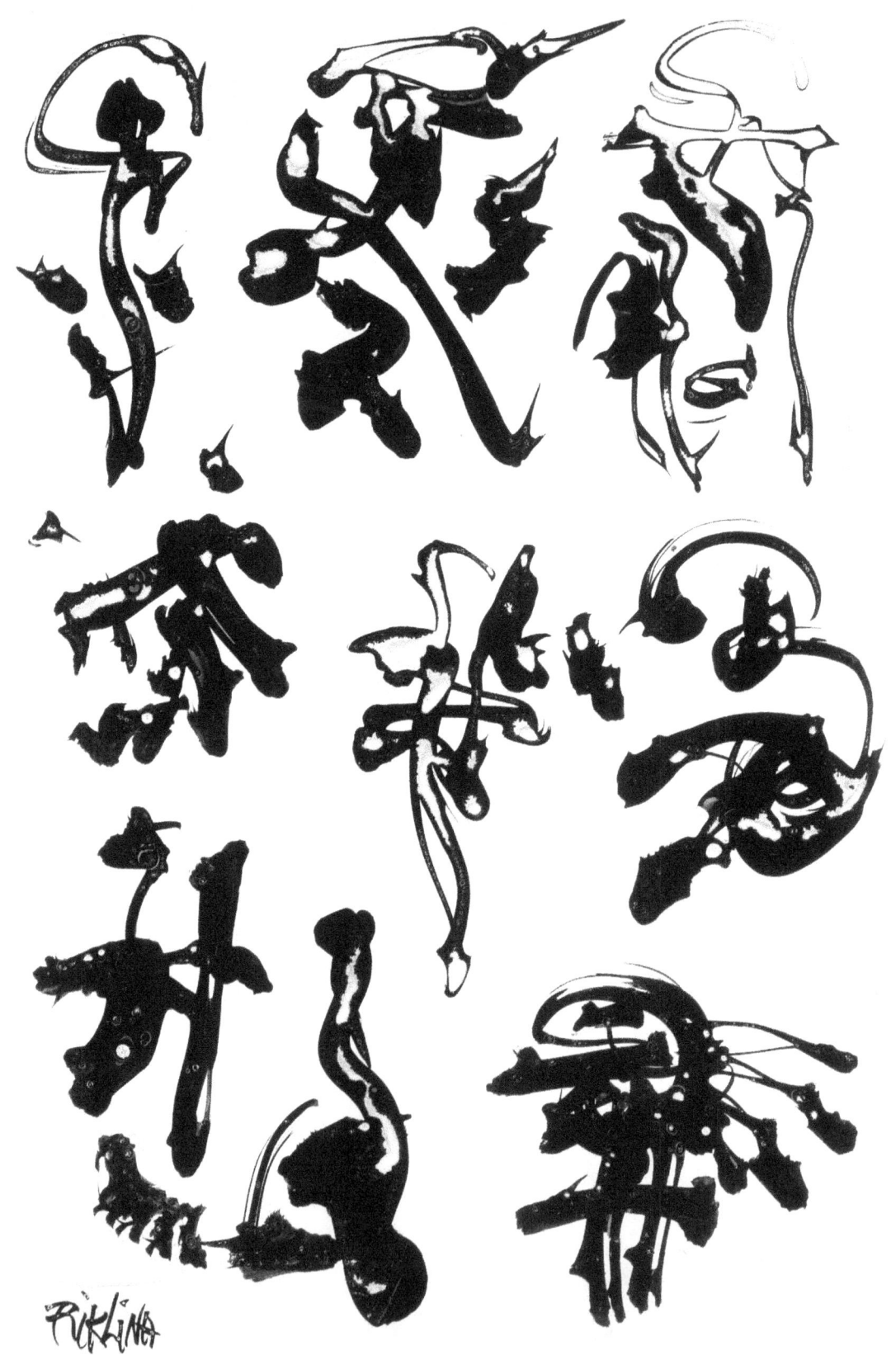

On Higher Phlogiston Current

"…the internal contradiction, extreme tension, and complexity in Césaire's imagery place him closer to the poetry of Artaud than to Breton."

–A. James Arnold

"Reason, I sacrifice you to the evening breeze"

–Aimé Césaire

Aimé Césaire

for Aimé Césaire

Your spirit
entranced by the scope of entangled scorpion moons
rising from the heights of flooded monsoon trees★

As if
in a pre-intestinal era
you consorted with the essence of trilobites★
with the essence of in-fluvial   lions
like an utterance from the cells

There existed as concurrence
a blinding amniotics
a lethal testing juncture
which you summoned like a bell
calling
the first grave dogs of Kemet★

& these grave dogs
bearers of wounds & theocracy
gave you
the first glimpse
the first hieratic imagination
of the way the stars were shifted at your birth

They gave you
the first ardour
the first nomadic dressing gowns
in which you appeared
magnified out of ether

At Basse-Pointe*
in a dwelling on Martinique
as the 2nd of six siblings*
crawling on rapacious sunbeams

It was you who heard Hugo
before falling asleep as an infant
it was you who learned the cascades of French
while ingesting volcanic eruption
it was you understanding
psychic transmixture & poverty
somehow knowing beneath your derma
the nervous glaciation of werewolves & owls

Yet within this brew of nascent baffling alchemics
Racine was unknowingly breached
Baudelaire & Villon
known from the overspill of the syllabus of Ronsard

In a curious sense
I do not acquire or acquiesce data
nor spend my moments imprinting mirages
because I know Aimé

that the Sun had prepared you for boldness ⋆
like the power of an irrefutable Pharoah
irregular with cubits & fathoms
having as your power a guided glycerin blinding
which led to new regions of water

At one level
a dark umbilical instrument
at another
pure concussives as expression
like a powerful theorem
active with fever & coding

As if
you always spoke to yourself
while glaring at a broken inquisitor's model

Then staging half-events in yourself
as if your mind always feasted at the cusp
of an enthralled uraeus

The body thus guided
as an incidental diamond
alive as a flash
enlivening
thankless circularity
without scattered aroma
drifting beyond its prism

Never the uncleansed hominidae
you were the mountainous guava
a scent seemingly drafted from lilies

Again I can only guess of a scent
randomly pulled out of lava
out of the dust of a flammable novae
not born of the dust of a scavenged bio-liquidity

A state
announced in your cells
as aqua dialogics
propulsive
as illusive underwater roads
leading to a luminescent level
which you occupied according to the laws
of a fulminate laterality
ignited on a map of scorching geometry
& the latter
Martinique
with the body of mongoose registrations
with its "hot moist" plains
burning with elements of intangible observations

Aimé
I surmise that the landscape was not a sum in itself
but the interactive plenum
between breathing
the gross advance of moss

& lightning from the cosmos

& I can add to this
bulletins of privacy & caimans

& a rookery of Macaw clouds consuming their own dimensions

So since the Sun was shifted at your birth ★
it harnessed curious consuming reaches
these singular orange & blue lightning's lightnings
& the triple rise of various optical effects

Because of these shifts
your mind conjoined with sapphire at star rise
which empowered in your case
the voice which blew through lenticular calderas
feasting on saburras
not unlike a sigil rattling around a sacrificial ark
which allowed you understanding through neural abasement
by basalt by necrotic pins
which allowed you advancement
through quickened funicular motion

The wounds you studied seemed impoverished & sullen
& your motion seemed to whirl inside a transparent lava
all the while rising like a bird from scaler infernos

To me
it is like seeing your shadow on an onyx cliff
& you knew this shadow through half wrought explosives

yet while in the maze of these kyphotic trances
there appeared Suzanne Rossi★
divine adrenaline
bouquet transmuted from the aura of lepers

& I admit
that these are sketches
personal assumptives on my part
as I seek to withstand your shadow in motion
your exhibited afflictions
seeking in their circumstance for meaningful advance
for restructuring bruised nopals
for understanding the perfect notion of intuitive trans-arrival

I take this as my way of subconsciously structuring
your metamorphic instants
your rivers
your sluices
the gathered fire in your darkness

No you were not the *nègre* from Martinique
nor the eminent raconteur
deciding from afar the calliopes & schisms
weighed as nouns in the yard of the Sorbonne

Of course you were the most redolent
the most hissing form of mist
the most uranian of scarabs
understood as interpreting menace
in the voice of Scorpion & Shabaka★

having in your system the first mental circuitry
of a bird maker
of an invisible delta of verbs
spilling as great incendiary wanderings
as insidious systems of grammar

If I call you a spectre from some old Roman cave urn
carved by verbal thinking dice
you could only laugh at my rumour
knowing it to be a pointless glandular beacon
a corrupted file pulled from old musical scores

& here you can understand
that I have created my sigil from a compost warren
from a fundamental sorrow
now rising as you've risen
into a strange combustible ozone
spiralling as the gist
of a strange planetary feeling
through fundamental seeing condensed by aurality

So for you
cadavers were never the copy of a copy partially settled in glass
or manoeuvered as reactive ash points
to be maniacally hidden
in non-existent convalescence
being withdrawn
& one by one
being broken in two on an isolated sandbar

You were never the sage
who was listless
who was moribund in Paris
seeking out mulatto salons
or pandering to elites with their malfunctioning bleakness

Instead you sought out the obstreperous
with Senghor & Damas
all of you soaked by telepathic kinetics

You recited sources of sources of sources within sources
emerging from your quarters
which was a crevice within the Sun

French for you*
was no obligatory error
no labourious domain
where you excelled
to show submission
to enact intellectual recension

For you it was nothing less than totalic instigation
a verbal tornado ploughing through ruptured wheat

French being nothing that dialysis could open
nothing that containment or reason could build

In 1937*
you cast the interstitial outlines
of water owls & skinks

always their vileness misleading with opprobrium
casting spells on the Rue Blanchot
by the dizziness of odour

I think of you in this seed form
mesmerizing daylight
making from brocade an armistice with monsters
in order to undermine the Pentecost
in order to feed more fuel into that which was heathen *

I agree
you attracted cecropias *
aurelian jellyfish trees
monoretic lions
strange dialysis gazelles

Prior to the Sino-Tibetan holocaust *
there was the storm off Martinique *
haunted by slavery
by transatlantic aggravation
reeling
when you returned from the continent
proto *Cahier* in hand
with Suzanne
holding in her bodice
a mixture of light
within an internal sea

She was taffeta
enriched by blue & incessant solar beams

by spun crystal
by delirious torches
& your cells upon her touch
seemed to always transmute to electrifying moonlight

Again
Martinique
newly spawned in the *Cahier*
with its stench
with no more than horses for its road cars
then its mills
its "hypoglossal" ditches
being what I gather it to have been
a genetic pornography
spilling like wild asters
burning like fire in endless "agoraphobia"

Martinique
a worn but grand baronial house
consumed "by petty hushed up scandals"
"by petty unvoiced guilts"
so the sum of the land was staggered by drainage
by undeciphered jiculi rushing up a stair of cinders
finding its world collapsed
as an unborn in-tenuity
not an incandescent Bordeaux★
not a rush of sanguineous complication
ignited by The Edict of Nantes

but a meaninglessness.
a hovel
sometimes lit up by the "tragic futilities"
of a "single noctiluca"

So I re-spawn the field *circa* 1937

The ruses in your speech
remained no more than proto-explosive

You had advanced from the *Lycée Louis-le-Grand*★
entangled in the flames of *L'Étudiant noir*★
with Damas
& Diop
& Ousmane Socé
along with Senghor
& magnetic racial topology
during your assiduous stay at *École normale supérieure*★

Then there was *Banjo*★
& Frobenius
& the rising of Africa beyond the mouth of racist regimes

By 1939
Cahier
the *Notebook*
Volontés

The electrified visitation
the power which scaled the *Tropiques*

Then you lectured on Rimbaud
& lit the halls of study
wavering as they were beneath the weight of colonial nerve regimes

You the unstable meteor
the skittish mist churning with intrigue*

For instance:
"caryophyllaceous"
"thumping…hernandia Sonora songs"
the above being dexterous verbal flicks
from old "chromosomian" hands

Your hands
which twitched with "scorpaena" daggers
were not unlike bound lizards
escaping from "Ursa Major"

& I think of colonization
of stolen silver & bodies
of a rarefied Africa captured
by the ice of dark volitional sorcery
the stark campaign of Europe*
which imprinted on our melanin a focused devastation
thus proving us a means to lean on self-hatred

Creating in us self-thought as the accursed
always posited by the sting of self-annulment
always casting our expression into doubt
into savage diagnosis

& you quite rightly accused them in your *Discourse* *
of bribery
of chaos
of lying
of unadorned distortion
of total hatred of deeper insight
the culture of Kemet under this regime
thrown on quite palpable slag

The European thought schematic
crude intervallic distortion
which allows me to strike out at the Hellenic Greeks
of the carvings at Samothrace
at the Parthenon
alive as intentional lessening

Hellenic Greece was not your reservoir of breathing
not your suit of burning carcasses

It remained for you poisoning by amnesial lucre

& this lucre
self-destructive centigrade
cold parabolas which glint
which cover up the Sun with untruth

Hellenic Greece:
divided in itself
a self-imperiled stasis
by a curious & regressive parallax
by haunted urge as anti-uranian kindling

Your spirit
Aimé
the pyramids
the first 7 dynasties of pyramidal production★
the original calculations at Lake Nyanza★
established learning at Wo-Se★

You being a perfect Hersetha★
igniter of Diop★
instructor on the mechanics of the trilobites
known monomial transmitter
of destroyed & resurrected conflagrations

I say
Césaire
voice from the valley of diamonds
as form from an unclaimed Orion
while all the while you slept in a subconscious sun

& such sleep always re-emitted ether
& became a remarkable endogeny unto itself

Thought for you
the hissing of jackals
the compound hissing of jackals
the compound seismology of sorcery as zeal
you being the old concocter
the mangrove viper
the plentified error
at a perfect conquest tree

Yet I cannot stand up in a pulpit
in harried professional disguise
announcing
strand by strand your 20 acts of treason
according to soliloquy by starvation
which translates in my mind
to your *Discourse*
where you argued
"that colonialism works to 'de-civilize' the colonizer"
"torture"
"violence"
"immorality"
inspire its coffers of the "abyss"
its maintenance of brutal salt & corruption
its havoc within internal order

& I suspect your phantom Nobel honours
were sabotaged by this writing
by its magnificent subversion
calling the Western Christians the inspirers of Nazis ★

Your *Discourse*
"a declaration of war"
a forthright challenging statement

First
you condemned Europe's honour as leprosy
you regrew fur on its face
caught in its lies as simulacra to itself

So

in your depth of depths

I feel you comparing it to the cubits of Luxor

to the stellae which professes eternity

over & over again

with Europe being no more than common statistical craft

mounted on the bones of fatuous consumption

Its result:

pillage by offending inferno

a consumptive & detailed mockery of achievement

with a Nordic saviour on its hands *

simply drowned in the longevity of its crimes

Consider its astonishing sanctions against life

its stunted biblical ire

where the body is brought down

& nailed

& worshipped

& made a priority for havoc

& you perfectly mocked

its non-incisionary subtext

as the person at lesser scale

being a subhuman Oedipus

a kindled mammoth in the Artic

Aimé

I can say that we know from both our sides

the odyssey of the lungfish

escaping to breathe air & then returning to its depths
to reattain the water vacuum

Again
we are more than bottom feeders ★
we are more than the poor nitrogen statistic
claiming for ourselves de-emphatic withdrawal
claiming for ourselves leisure through clandestine misnomer

No
Aimé
we are not depressed
we are the energy of dark & gold
of that wonder which breathes through the anarchic
constructing sun warrens
making through blizzards of water
revelations of new account

Harassed & known as disadvantaged tree life
we've come to announce from the combinatory plane
a "superior order"
as new & unstained ghosts
combining both life & death
through the oxygen of delirious "droseras"

Now we are running hidden in a swamp
like couriers for revengeful Indians
carrying invisible moons
filled with precarious poisons
with undozing iguanas

with the beautiful messenger ostrich
with the "acacia" of extortion

& you
with the hissing & the blood songs
leading the way through imperiled "lumbar" serpents
with me
never thinking you are dead

Igniting our steps on the "glass of high noon"
you inspire in me the crazed captain
oneirically flying in his cellar at dawn

You inspire in me deliberate jonquil elevation
diagrams of perfect mongrel sharks
of red & white horses flanked by the inconceivable

You've convinced me
even in your present state
that I am no longer a blood dwarf
that I have never been a blood dwarf
subverting the angle of in-feral Medusae

I look to you across the distance of death with depth
understanding my own portrait
with green roses in my eyes

Therefore my cyclonic "solstice"
hails you
treats you
& treats your power as foremost ascent

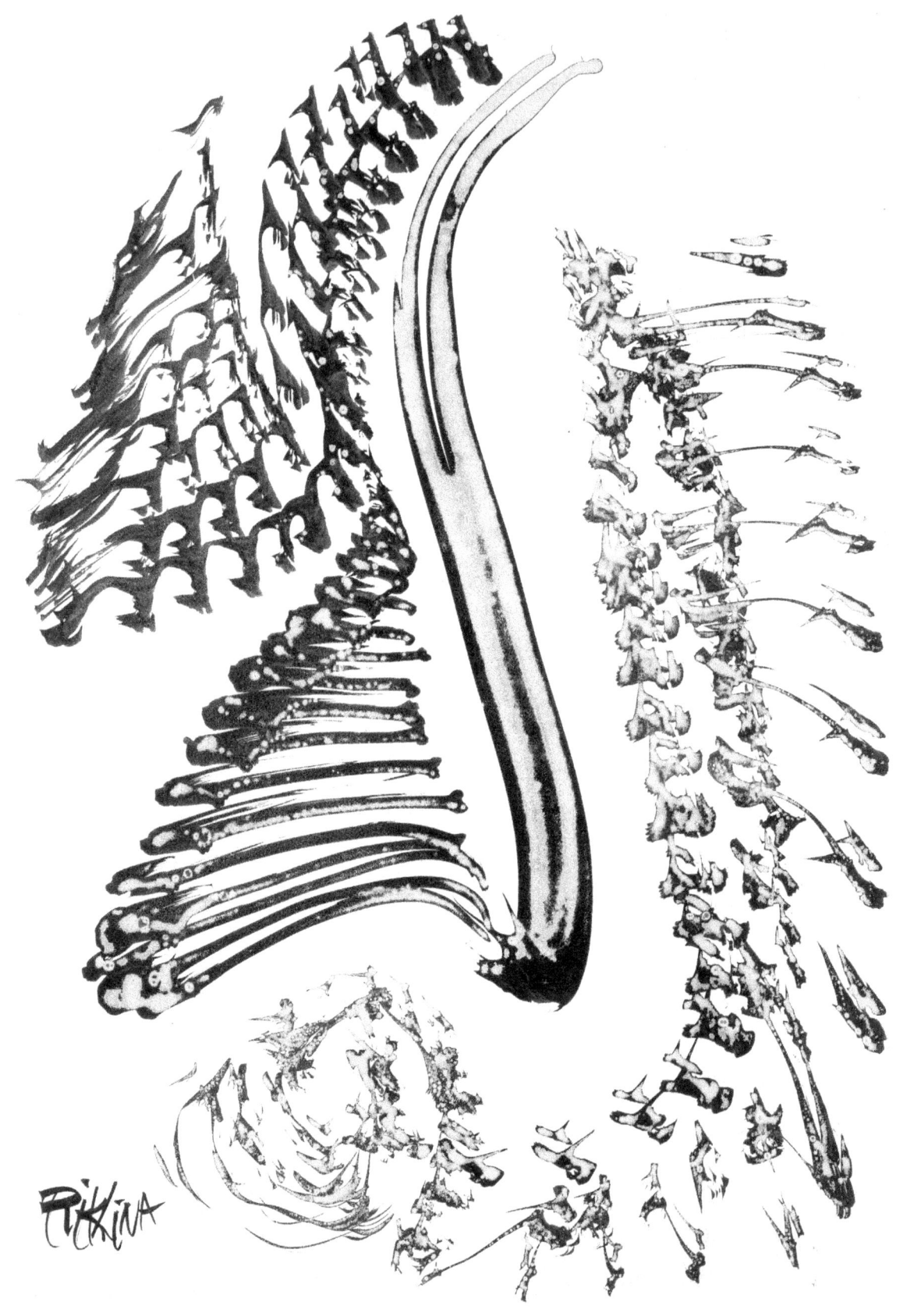

When I think of your poems
I feel *Velocity*
& the interactive forces
of scapegoats & harems

Again
I think of guttering candles & disclosure
of feral canopies housed with faces

& as you have said
there is the "anophelic" future
the hissing of a globalistic compass
like blazing light on a futuristic sea

& it is not going too far to say
that we are juxtaposed elements along the lines of infinity
knowing in essence the cold of black star groups
their seismic neon riddles
their unctuous & captivating wind flames
that go blank

& at the same time they light up the Earth
like scattered moths
as if all the sea lanes were blurred
with the scorched activity of land brought to sea

Knowing that this was the Earth testing
your failed aggregation
your first failed stint at the *École normale*
when your poetry first blazed
when your health went to seed

& then fatherhood

& the first germinal glints which flared from the *Cahier*

1939

August

Volontes

I am now repeating your first enfevered background

repeating a crucial period in your ascent

as you brought new struggles into view

According to the Brown shirts

you raised criminals into potentates

they being of high African renown

verbally arraying them in unearthly métier

Again the *Cahier*

with its intense lenticular salt

with its brazen phonemic parallels

with its doves conjoined to the very notion of monsters

Certainly not a poem which raises its head

from pronounced procedural lodging

but from alluvial dust

taking strange momentums from bribery

like a gestural hawk in its apocalyptic bodice

The *Cahier* hoisted

the central fire of vilification

in order to revalorize its heat of European derogation

walking over the xanthochroidal image

with its witchdoctor's footprints
with its burning demonstration
taking apart all the ridicule heaped upon us

Aimé
we have been slandered
then accused of possessing faulty simian's constrictives
accused of breathing by embarrassment
of ambling by means of "sea urchin spines"
kept away from the White ideal
by means of "bamboo hooks"

For you
European limitation was dazed
an obliterate claustrophobia
under the guise of cerebral simulacra
in the deepest sense aspiring
to reductive solar absorption

& Aimé
I am not writing to praise the *Cahier*
with drafts of new oxygen
with an incoherent glossary
seeking for new subversion
praising your result
with indefatigable stasis
in-organically possessed by isometric krill

There is danger in such halted assessment

I could place your flaws in my hand
& break them
& scatter broken advice
making it linger through ghosts
in undeveloped refrains

Of course I am truly speaking to your spirit
to your extinguished presence
now rising out of sleep

& I am not saying this
to exercise depravity
or to make myself known
according to theatrics
or the dictates of alienation

No
I am not a thief who wanders
through insurrectional gullies
always blessing himself with morose bubonics

This writing is not scaled
to the glossary of the metropolis
to the self scaled-down
to a cavalry of warrens
graceless
de-revelatory
wallowing in horrific calumny

I say my action taken
is far beyond a seasonal de rigueur

beyond an advanced copy of itself
promoting the text through delimited eschatology
through a charisma of secularity
uncertain of your language
never knowing its power as an amazing decalcomania*
as a riveting solar internality

No
personal supposition could never confine me
according to a base or deleterious understanding

Because Aimé
you remain a shadow which looms & disrupts the Occident
like a wasp which leaps from a coruscating juniper
enlivening in your wake a misanthropic ozone

& so I say *stretto*
the overlapping voice
which sings to itself according to tornadic placement

Again the *Cahier*
as bottomless
as stunned & oracular happenstance

According to your purview
the negative has been empowered
through xanthrochroidic confabulation
they who have sabotaged
they who have drawn portraits of self-hatred of themselves
& through the ruling of their image of God
they who have pronounced as sustained conclusion

the rational voice

throughout their mechanistic compound

A compound

with the scar of a poisonous tercet

with its suppressive psycho-emotional ensemble

in contradistinction

you possessed an injudicious sauntering

having exuded your sound by indelible ocarina

where no seeming pattern concurred

where no outcome proceeded in regulated manner

No

your voice by rasping

your voice by deviation

like a scorpion trail across unfixed memoranda

as I reach your "equable casuarinas" *

your "unloosed…monsters" full of sweeping conflagration

If I can speak in terms of red orchids

of blue & unbalanced cataracts

I can somehow start to circle you

so as to transmute new negations

overcoming oblique & colourful depravities

to stress nuance

to stress alchemical crops

in the form of an unburdened wheat

Perhaps I can call myself a crow

screeching from a tower of destroyed centavos

because I understand
your insurrectional codes
in susurrant earthquake tremor
always unnerving the travel goer
the Occidental populist with his minstrels of bad phrasing

As you naturally understood
their concerns which torment the spirit
which brew in the stomach as anthrax & vertigo

& above all you knew
that torment can brew
& re-arise from the soil as suffocated panthers

May I speak of 1941
of your "open letter" to the "local Catholic prelate" *
concerning the form of collaborationist crime
concerning the Church as Hitler's death bride
concerning Pius & his sojourn under Vichy ideology
you who sparked René Étiemble
with your devastating unions
with your unbarred fangs
with your pungent documentation

The Church:
a racist soil
an empty conjugation

An institution at the source of your critical capital
with its fish & its cross amidst dubious advocating

of Christ at its doorstep
handing out flails & bubonics
handing out jaundiced scales from the firmament
knowing in this handing out
that the angels sing badly
that they are molten conjugal dwarfs
singing on behalf of a swarm of oily concubines
as though he had delivered delirious lace or ivory

This writing being to you antithetical to Cortez
who stood at "the top of the great teocalli" ★
or to "Pizarro before Cucos"
commanding "helmets"
& "lances"
& "cupidities"
their strategies always called for deafening instigation
for planned connivance
for orchestrated greed

& yes Aimé
they've continued to rape the world
with an animated blood stick
with hellish weaponry by iron

& never did you speak these thoughts
from the prurient norm of an armchair
or from comfortable means provided by assent ★

No Aimé
it remained your referendum

that the spectacular was unfounded in reason
that the breaking down of nervous slaughter
was always bad for the capital system

Just 2 of your advances
one: ingesting oxygen rays
& the latter: emitting jungles of green matter

Simple
unstained
without the barrier of guilt

Even in death you remain in media res

Aimé
can I say that you are active & remain
a ship across explosive "sea swamps"
with haunted barrier gulls overhead
knowing in your travels
"rain"
serpents
"fear"
cacophony?

Knowing at times that living
transpires through "lingering ambiguity"
through night salts with their quavering
through unlit penumbras which linger inside a desert

Without knowing Aimé
this remains the aqueduct in midair

the gainful vibratory suffix

the compassionate form without populated manger

this being Fort-de-France by unintended findings

which is not an ideology condemned to votes & shackles

but a conjurated zone

a scorched imaginary powder with clairaudient castles

alive with strange cerulean announcements

& these are not the castles of "Queen Blanche of Castille" ⋆

but castles above the sound which trembles

with horrific noun count

having risen above the sway of regressive jurisprudence

This is not to say that the ozone is rife with centaurs

or evolution has been scaled to higher phlogiston current

But let me say Aimé

that the ozone is as if flooded with sunspots

with oracular grammar

with fulgurating gerunds

& we both know

this is no longer history

rankled by egregious raconteur

by devastator's boosting

repeating itself over & over by means of rancorous hegemony

& for this past millennia

this hegemony

under the European skills of a dehydrated armour

A dehydration so vast
that it attacks & reattacks
its own engenderment as human

So when you spoke for the Sun
when gazelles conjoined with secret parallels of starlight
energy concurred
conjunction was not infected with the arrogance of killing

So one cannot say
that such a contrast is didactic
one dimensional
sullied
reductive

You understood these concerns
at the highest sensitivity
that any maroon could emit

Because you could have it no other way
than returning blows against the blood hunters
which was saturate in the *Discourse*
when you spoke of fauna left askew
when you spoke of eyes put out in Madagascar★

& quite rightly
everywhere they've been
blood loss
treachery
whispering

& this whispering concludes

that we are buried below the human

that we are less than an imperfect creature

that we are conjurers who rob ourselves bare

& I say this as your indelible compadre

who corroborates with the fire inside your ethos

who hallucinates sigils & carries them to outer society

So by psychic storage

by bursts of rainfall

by interior tracing

we conclude upon the Sun which is Africa

which add to all the cubits which is 9★

which is an atmosphere which is plentiful

Yet it can be also announced

that all its power has been converted

to exhaustive degradation

to disabled internment

to alcoholic sheets so conversant with the day traders

So when the ozone thins Aimé★

we will breathe

when the floods astonish

we will swim

when the nebulae scorch sands

we will float

inside our melanotic essence

genetically twined to the first known balance of the cosmos

I am speaking Aimé

of our great absorptive features

of our signals which embody the light year

making contact with billions of habitable Earth zones★

within the density of local star groups

knowing that we are seedlings

ores

principates

You being a pioneer of motility

helping me overcome the distraction of cerebral compendia

so that I now call to you

floating above a strange meandering death heap

& no one can conceal

that the call is not real

or that the soil has not been brightened

it is the direct indivisible eye

the bounteous light

of pure electrical heightening

Electrification being the circuitous transfer

between energy & heaven

this being the BA★

the "unified"

the immortal ray which links the planes

Then the "motion" & "emotion"

through the purity of its Akashic state

thus

I understand your post-mortality
drifting as it is
through the Valley of Giants
your voice not unlike the codes which ascend through
    "Tasmanian" opera

Your voice now operant
as "circumvolution"
as "fulvous" glance
as mediumistic shimmer

A syntax understood by creatures
in a swap of green water
in a castle of ferocious cacti
in a depth of luminous calderas

If I am listening to your shadow
it is because I am prone to you through telepathic integer
through your nomos of royalty
governing by vibration
in a heightened python city

& of course
this is not talk about a statistical codex
or redoubled economies
or even harvested rum through illegal yield
no
but I'm thinking instead of leopards who speak through trees
or darkened vanishing owls
& there can be no question about the source of your make-up

personally giving as proof

the outer ringlets of Saturn as absorbed in your name

An alterity

predatory anaphora

totally unlike the "Western" mind

where life is viewed as a superior burden

as pointless obligation

where the "death of the body is death of the mind"

where "no superior power" exists "beyond man"*

The latter

an ignited kindling

a flaw

a blazeless harrowing debasement

a nervous moral precipice

a tersely functioning moral disorder

burning with a vile & in-salient oppositional fury

achieving when it can

corruption through physical particulate

This being the source of your rupture with Aragon* & Thorez*

the latter holding on to terms

utilitarian with mis-assessment

as if in Martinique

as if the populace was beholden to itself through European
    termination

Aimé

as if you were the subjective dilettante

the Communist
as a brittle but darkened straw
watered by the blood of Stalin & his lepers
& Thorez & his ilk as dominant censors of the era
who attempted to lock you into their view
through embarrassing White paternalism
who attempted to code your voice as deaf electrical knowledge

In a word:
useless
like Arabian soil parched by poisoned maize

In your presence
Aragon would bristle
with his thoughts shredded
as if you called for his ouster from the Party
by means of votes gathered in hermetic Amsterdams
in telepathic Pragues
in scenarios of an unclaimed Paris

You created in their minds
the substance of arcane locales
they shivered
they sought your non advancement
they sought your allegiance as a non-evolving sycophant
& both of them
Aragon & Thorez
modeling themselves on non-evolving tertiary tools
as if you had risen to the level of their abstracted approval

Yet you spoke to Aragon in a tone
above the boulevard of the herd
with the power of seeming indirection
as an amorphic insurrectionist
as a pointless mystical scholar
with your scientific reason denuded by dyslalia

& you knew Aimé
in your spirit of spirits
the Communist debacle
with its distortions & malfeasance
with its spread of worms
with its unconscionable enactment
of the greatest amount
for the greatest abstract amount
& for all of this
a wooden cup earned
intermittent mutton
a bag of stale bread

& over & above this
Martinique
an isolate cultural mass
without voudou steeds
without the shamanistic Congo

& this is what you emitted to Thorez
concerning Stalinist lore as a disemboweled thesis
the interposition of the Stalinic apparatus

Knowing the above as you knew it
was nothing more than a scar without imploded nuance
a criteria without the power for casting spells
always creating ridicule for the moat of the unseen
this being communism through Thorez
with his unspinning sun
anachronistic & blazeless

Such speech unrelated to osmotics
to angular foretelling
to the transmuted instant
instead there is the bureaucratic thumbprint
language reduced to docile palpability

& quite rightly as you stated
the Martinican particular rose above this double maw
of classification & killing
of the moon as a transfixed altercation

For you Aimé
this was the condoned sanctioned as movement
which multiplied any thought beyond rote
as unserviceable & beyond the concrete

Having known blue winter suns
having glimpsed your powers lingering in the snow
allowed you perseverance through alienation
by the fact of your exposure to nothingness

& again & again from the unseasonable
from the inferno of the seeming inferior

you've arisen again & again from unplagiarized aggregation
in order to promulgate the wayward
in order to triumph through the troubles of scorched blessings

This was the atmosphere
the party bosses
who attempted to herd you
who sought alignment with the masses through metric procedure

For them
your expression obscured the masses
was a matter of mis-arrangement
always seeking to track down your words
like escaped grains of salt

They sought to register your complaints
as oblivious dossiers
as edicts conjoined by elitist imperfection
but they were nothing more to you
than cadavers boiled in thickened saliva
nothing more than indignity confined with complication
with you casting riddles within the outlines of Africa
more alien to them than Jupiter
more arresting than mountain chains on Phobos

For you
the body inside the body
was the fount of living anima
a conflagrant depth
which transmuted soils from all unstable suns

Thus Martinique
being water which gurgled in a leper's voice
with its codes of mountainous gnawing
with its uncanny sprawling
savouring the baleful
the clairvoyant minerals
the liminal conjurations
aptly perceived by Breton through his inklings

I mean his utter intuition
which incessantly enthralled
which surreptitiously engendered the purity of incessance

Which was dice turning in invisible fauna

Or hypotheses rent by fuel in destabilized pre quanta

Always motility
always the thought of pure lakes
advancing through cells
these being floods you called the contradictive rapids
the inner hurricane spinning as un-subtended motion

So the cosmos became the multiple & particular of itself
exploding & thawing
as a unified connivance
breathing at a rate which the rectilinear could never know

& you were at one with its breathing
at a level which eclipsed the carnivore's portion
yet which you understood as being the hot moist ciphers of
    Martinique

with its plains
with its incandescent crops
with its burning gulls
with its circumferential clouds
with its beatific harbour at Fort-de-France

If I were to cast you as a ghost in the role of an enigmatic pangolin
or as an unsculpted wolf with a sceptre
I could on the one hand balance your sculptings
or succumb to their ruthless technical concealment
never allowing myself
human flaw or shading
when approaching your monodic syllabication

As you've said
"My horse...hopscotched in rust"
the "Phoronidea...making roads with their tentacles"*
being odd rotative conjoinments
like an "amphisbaena" which flares*

This being the energy of your particular monodics
of its brute metabolics of colour
which continue to twist & explore
over & beyond the moods which ignite through alchemical paranoia
which remains subconscious lucidity
which remains a self-condensing peril understood

For instance
a meteor's light "in the Colocasia meadows"*
being 3 moons bluing above a lake of "undozing iguanas"

These are oddities I've culled
as if peering through a feral treatise on baiting
so I greet you ¾ way in half-light
shrouded
insecticidal
forming along the way
random erasures in my body

& these erasures
like a flood of maniacal blazes
appearing & disappearing
aleatoric with residue
so much so
that I breathe with your residue through English
knowing that we have surmounted the anglophobia of my glare
so that we are surrounded by consciousness
not unlike cosmic mountaineers on Miranda★

Mountaineers
who dwell outside gravitational ironics
outside the grammatical bounds of verbal didactics
being analogous to clouds as non-repetitive figurines
scattered & condensed as phosphenes
as occulted bravado
as vibrational assemblage
furious with unencumbered embarking

These are powers Aimé
not equated to accessible density

to banking with its rancid exchanges
seeking to configure an underhanded budget
according to glyphs sustained by bleak diurnal reports

At this level of assessment
Marx could never provide for us
with nothing beyond pure raiment
making us nothing more than comrades enacting their powers
through ideological submission

& I know Aimé
these are bygone issues
bygone relations
which spewed darkness
which spewed an empirical perspective on calamity
always fighting evolvement with a tuneless embrace

But you by allowing a riotous social inherence
you negated old budgets & rioted outside the law
having left a monitored economy
having dispersed with curt behavioural phrasing
prone with sketches of the understandable mean

Under the old regime Aimé
a cave was always filled with stubborn cortical donkeys
with a welter of frozen mongoose understanding
with general deflationary motion
which were not drills to hold the cerebral inside its cave
but unplanned tensions
dissonant behaviours

I'm thinking of Martinique
as a violent imaginary field
like the forces which collapse inside a blind dendritic mural
forged from human electrical current
humming in rivers of black erasure

I'm surmising this was your mind
with your wayward scarps
with your strange conducting pyre
wandering through concussive lagoons
beneath the fires of heightened imaginal sorties

Saying all of this
I do not propose to know all the perplexities of your depth
with its hallucination by heresy
with its scope by in-grown centigrade

I know that I concur with its leaps
with its susurrant variations
which has allowed true gain in my being
which has allowed the untoward to give birth to my thinking
as charismatic utility
where creatures ignite & consume their own fertility
which means hybridity
form & non form
conscripting the dialectical phase to the level of the uncertain
thus
the poetic charge
the rhythmos of bravery

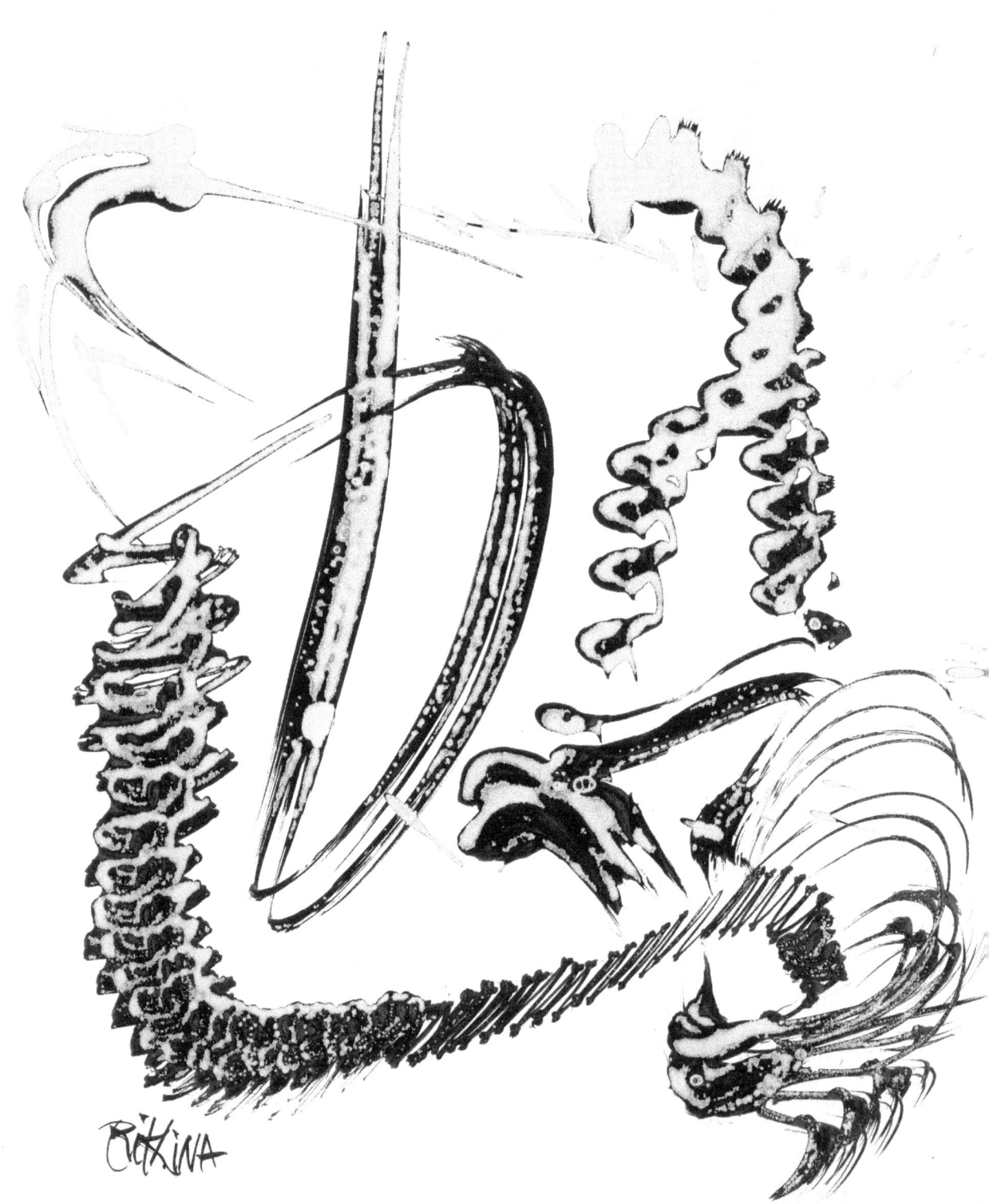

So when I utter your language
hurricanes seethe
glass shutters break
arroyos break in half

I call this Afric quanta
omniscient vibratory snares

For you
language was distance
conjoining in melanotic snares
in hyphenated postures
in "hyphenated" embrasures
but not an argument woven
from soulless stationary derma
but understanding the body through interactive tumult

Can I say in passing
that you remain the argonaut absorptive with apogees
with errata which rises as solarity
as sporulation across magical psychic expanse
which includes cosmic nopals
Olmec incunabula*
audible blessings?

Aimé
permit me to laterally spin circles
to go about my business without defending myself
so as to know you again & again
without problems condensed through expectation

Because of this
you arrive again from Po Tolo*
from a shift in magnetics
so as to arise from another kind of strength
without codes which misconstrue fate by terrestrial limit

& you know such things having had converse with light
incredibly streaking through mazes
bending & slurring like your words
across the white sands of the invisible

& I am not speaking of some capricious roundelay
or error combined through tragic mystical dearth
but of Divine concordance
beyond the normative blanks fueled by deduction

To the Nordic sensibility
you are "heat"
& "anger"
& sand
you are electric & viral
linked by arsenic through complication
being a tar-like vulture wading in urine

Your diametrics darkened by seeming moral delay
your optics pointing to perspicacious dishonour
to pointless ganglia as drift
this being your lingering accusation
against Greco-Roman disservice
who strategized on a warped colonial plank
within the fumes of a complicated syndrome

Their remains:
biased

Their thought:
savage & incomplete

Thus their humanism wanes beneath a fragmentary shield
"sordidly racist"
always announcing with a molten lisp
with a lingering geriatrics
taut with obstructional chaos
being custodial
invasive
extrinsic

They are the dazed
whom attempt & reattempt
to inspire by their invasions
in-benign dementia
regressive stochastics
so that the fate of the invaded
becomes a zone of confused holdings

Yet you knew & always
knew that the mirage of colonial mechanics
would become to see its face
as a sum of famished torpor trees with its eroded flanks
with its germinating postures
sinking in the depths of a bottomless photometry
inauspicious with mortality

As you peer from alterity

the cycle is reversed & these colonial mechanics follow you

across shattered fields of the spirit

forced to exile themselves to deafening & disappearance

which is not a march to import slaves

or to poach bauxite from the innards of Guinea

Aimé

this is not the zone of the biography of osmosis

but the macerated glare of beings

of fallen kindling

useless to themselves

more & more void of the power to stagger & kill

to convey across the world an aplanatic reign

The group you described in 1950

as greedy bankers

as "subservient bankers"

as "check-licking politicians"

with their "rigged investigations"

with "tendentious speculations"

with their pointless rational swans

lifted from tainted water

& so Aimé

I take a few strands of news

on the eve of the fall of the xanthochroids

plunging markets

"over bought" stocks

"nervous investors"

No longer the disinfected stones of racial ideology
or the acclimatized portion
splintered with profit by malfeasance

No Aimé
you know & I know
from both our different planes
that the art of being burns by bluish celestial dust
above nocturnally active "mountains"
like an agitated Eagle
or a winged azalea radiant with "mandibles"

Not thought as vermicular fungi
nor as disempowered silt
of deafened electrodes in the hills

No we are speaking through a blinded macular frame
through a disingenuous solar operation
scrawling out numbers from a disordered comet

Again
not the troubles of a fumeric arrow
moving as if astride an imbalanced mount
igniting its way through a gorge of claustrophobia

Because our eyes can see through African solar foil
we are privy to solar codex fountains
to igniferous hurricanes by sign

Not a stained nor blazeless square
but the circle which blurs & spins

which lifts and sustains the Earth
through the powers of mesmeric calendrics

Not the power provided by principle rote
but the sustained digestion of the evidence
mounted
through healthful physical laterality
charting open by the body as ray
by rampant daybreak in utopia
by cornucopia as cellular trans vicinity

Aimé
a blue uranian breathing
an unnamed flight by agreement
such are your poems
with their nitric shifts
with their cellular wisdom

They are levels beyond levels
spiraling without the haze of nostalgia

Let me say:
utterance
a beehive of camels
pulmonic lynxes
a hive of scorching spectra

Not a refusal to sway events
or a blistering methane form
or an explosive undermix gone bad

Let us raise our gnosis to hypabyssal consequence
to a sculpted mare as biochemical goddess
balanced by opaque weight
speeding across indigo & saffron

It is understood Aimé that sound in proto Sumerian
creates crystal
creates a riverbank of forms
through grammatical trace
through trans-suggestive balance
so that a syllabus of markings
takes place in the endlessness of camphor

It is you
who dug into the source of these first understandings
it is you who understood these first personifications of figment

So when you spoke of Christophe⋆
or hounded the behaviour of Caillois⋆
or merged with Damas & Lumumba
there was always the fact of Afric melanocity
dialectically opposed to the horror of its public ranking

In the afterworld
you continue to possess the in-sclerotic
the unnerving fingers
always astride your snarling nightmare pony

Glossary for
On Higher Phlogiston Current

<u>Monsoon trees</u>—"The months between June and November when Martinique is prone" to heavy rains and monsoons. p. 164

<u>Trilobites</u>—Earliest known group of arthropods. They appeared in the early Cambrian 526 million years ago and became extinct at the end of the Permian 250 million years ago. p. 164

<u>the first grave dogs of Kemet</u>—Salukis were the royal dogs of Kemet and one of the "oldest dog breeds in existence." Their breed have been found "mummified alongside the bodies of Pharaohs in the pyramids." It was in the 18th dynasty that they rose to prominence. Kemet is the name of ancient Egypt in its original African tenor. It means Black soil and Black people. p. 164

<u>Basse Pointe</u>—Birthplace in Northern Martinique of Césaire. "…his mother was a dressmaker and his father held a minor bureaucratic post as a tax inspector." p. 165

<u>as the second of six siblings</u>—"Aimé was the second of six children. His family's way of life was that of the rural poor, but the level of education of both his father and paternal grandfather as well as his father's status as a functionary set them apart and provided the children with a nurturing environment in which being Black and being French were not perceived as conflicting aspects of existence." p. 165

<u>that the Sun had prepared you for boldness</u>—In an interview with Charles Rowell during the early 1980's, Césaire made a point to note that Breton had taught him the virtue of boldness. He had also expressed the same fact in a much earlier interview years prior to this. p. 166

<u>So since the Sun was shifted at your birth</u>—Césaire was born under the sign of Cancer. Cancerians are prone to "considerable literary, artistic or orational content"… all of which marked the character of Césaire. p. 168

<u>Suzanne Roussi</u>—Wife of Aimé Césaire, born in 1913 in Trois-Îlets, Martinique. A philosophy student in the Paris of the 1930's, Suzanne, along

with Aimé, was interested in issues of identity, colonialism, alienation assimilation, and consciousness. A unique writer in her own right, she co-founded with Césaire the revolutionary journal *Tropiques*. p. 169

<u>in the voice of Scorpion & Shabaka</u>—Scorpion (early 32nd century BC?) was thought to be the first or an early leader of Ta Seti, the Nubian nation which existed south of Kemet, and which was the first recorded nation on Earth. Shabaka (late 8th century BC) succeeded in preserving Egypt's independence from outside foreign powers, especially the Assyrian Empire under Sargon II. Both of these two leaders in my mind represent nobility and ferocity, apt characteristics for Aimé Césaire. p. 169

<u>French for you</u>—Jean-Paul Sartre has mentioned that "Surrealism, a European movement in poetry, has been stolen by a Black man" (Césaire) "who turns it against them and gives it a well-defined purpose." p. 171

<u>In 1937</u>—A transitional year for Césaire, who was making his first steps into legend. Having completed the gruelling exams at the École normale supérieure, all the while continuing to work on his revolutionary *Cahier*. Also it was the year proto to the birth of his first child Jacques. p. 171

<u>in order to find more fuel into that which was heathen</u>—For Aimé and Suzanne Césaire poetry was "excess, immoderation, study of the forbidden, in the great blind drumming, the unbreathable absolute vacuum..." (Aimé, quoting an oration of Lautréamont.) As Suzanne says specifically, "From among the powerful war machines the modern world now places at our disposal... our audacity has chosen surrealism..." Instinctual language registration. p. 172

<u>Cecropias</u>—Dioecious tropical trees. p. 172

<u>the Sino-Tibetan holocaust</u>—Chinese invasion of Tibet, 1950. p. 172

<u>Martinique</u>—Colonial Martinique was initiated by Columbus and "making the region known to European interests," from his first charting of the island in 1493, to his introduction, in 1502, of pigs and goats to its confine. "In 1635, Cardinal Richelieu created the...Company of the Isles of America...The company contracted with Messers l'Olive and Duplessis to occupy and govern on its behalf the Caribbean islands." p. 172

<u>Bordeaux</u>—Symbol of the rich northern nations which Césaire psychically occupies in the *Cahier* when he orates "My name is Bordeaux and Nantes

and Liverpool / and New York and San Francisco / not a corner of the world but carries my thumb print and my heel mark on / the backs of the skyscrapers and my dirt…Who can boast of having more than I?" It is like he is a ghostly Hannibal who has reinvaded the North.   p. 174

Lycée Louis-le-Grand—School which Césaire and Senghor attended during the early 1930's. "…a public secondary school located in Paris widely regarded as one of the most rigorous in France." It is a school which has produced a bevy of influential personalities from Césaire to the Marquis de Sade, to Sarte, to Voltaire.   p. 175

L'etudiant Noir—A publication which Césaire "started in Paris with fellow students Léopold Senghor and Léon Damas," as well as with Gilbert Gratiant, Leonard Sanville and Paulette Nardel. *L'etudiant Noir* contains Césaire's first published work "Nègreries" which is notable not only for its disavowal of assimilation as a valid strategy but also for its reclamation of the word *nègre* as a positive term.   p. 175

École normale supérieure—The École Normale Supérieure (ENS) is a French elite institution of higher learning. It was conceived in 1794 during the French Revolution and later reorganized by Napoleon. The ENS has two main sections, literary and scientific, which provide a platform for students to pursue high-level careers in government and academia.   p. 175

Banjo—Claude McKay's novel published in 1929 concerns the episodic adventures of Banjo (Lincoln Agrippa Daily) and his roving band of fellow sailors, Ray, Larnah, Bugsy, always in and out of trouble around the docks of 1920's Marseilles, but with this difference, it is steeped in an undertow of Garveyism and Black consciousness.   p. 175

the skittish mist churning with intrigue—Césaire was never prone to working with preset codes or standards, which includes surrealist codes or standards. One can then truly appreciate his rejection of the French Marxists, documented in his letter to Maurice Thorez, the latter a Communist bureaucrat, whom Césaire accuses of myopia when confronted with the needs of people of colour.   p. 176

the stark campaign of Europe—The relentless assault on Africa commenced by the Portuguese from the early to late 1400's was not only concerned with the establishment of riches, but also with the psychological devastation ingrained in the African, which has always accompanied all material acquisition.   p. 176

Discourse—Césaire's famous *Discourse on Colonialism*, penned in 1950, remains a trenchant attack on European values. It sums up these values into a negative equation of greed, violence, and institutional self-debasement.
p. 177

the first 7 dynasties of pyramidal production—According to Asa Hilliard "It was during the first seven dynasties that most of the pyramids were built." It might be added that these were the pure African dynasties.
p. 178

Lake Nyanza—Lake Nyanza, part of "the western branch of the Rift Valley," which "runs in a great arc through the Great Lakes region where humanity first emerged and evolved its original knowledge base."
p. 178

Wo'se—Original name of Luxor/Thebes.
p. 178

Hersetha—"...teachers of mysteries" in ancient Egypt. There were "Mystery Teachers of Heaven" (astronomy, astrology), "Mystery Teachers of All Lands" (geography), "Mystery Teachers of the Depths" (geology, cosmography), "Mystery Teachers of The Secret Word" (philosophy, theology), and the School (mystery) of "Pharaoh and Mystery Teachers" (language, law, communications).
p. 178

Diop—Referring to Cheikh Anta Diop (1923-1986) who emigrated to Paris in 1946. It was Diop's contact with Césaire which ignited Diop's life direction. A direction which was consumed in casting scientific proof concerning the origination of world knowledge in Africa. Diop originally went to Paris to study physics. During his stay Diop translated parts of Einstein's *Theory of Relativity* into his native Wolof. Diop's education included history, physics, Egyptology, linquistics, anthropology, economics and sociology. Not content with the aforementioned he was also politically active in the RDF, the *Rassemblement Démocratique Africain*.
p. 178

calling the Western Christians the inspirers of Nazis—This, I surmise, was the last straw which snapped a great divide in the Nobel committee. Ernst Renan, in Césaire's equation, is the equal of 19th century racist Gobineau. It is on record that the Nazis were not averse to the influence gained from observing the racial practices of the American South. For instance, between 1920 and 1923 there was an average of 50 African-Americans lynched per year.
p. 179

with a Nordic saviour on its hands—In the hands of the Europeans Jesus Christ has become an Anglo-Saxon figurine operant in the vernacular mind as the king of life and death.
p. 180

we are more than bottom feeders—Black people are gifted with invisible levels of psychic grasp demeaned and negatively altered by left brain dominance and its expertise concerning mechanical implementation. In the case of R.A. Schwaller de Lubicz' study of the temple at Luxor, he writes in *The Temple of Man* that "mathematics have demonstrated the existence of elements that fall outside the physical." The Roman/Western mind seems inevitably stifled when it comes to evaluation in these regions of palpability. To the modern material mind these are the unanswerable areas still underscored by discredit. And it must be understood that the "Temple" at Luxor, the apex of Schwaller's study, was constructed by Black people. p. 181

your first failed stint at the École normale supérieure—It was during this period that Césaire was plagued by a contractive turmoil in his system—pulling away from French values yet at the same time forced to imbibe them for daunting exams as he attempted to earn his teaching credential. All of this took place as his first writings were beginning to bloom. This, due to the nervous strain, put Césaire's health on precarious footing; the above occurred during the middle of the 1930's. p. 184

decalcomania—The technique of transferring an image from "specially prepared paper" onto another sheet. I am thinking in this regard of the Spanish surrealist painter Óscar Domínguez and in specific reference to one of his many "untitled" images of a fantastic lion caught in full stride. Discovered by Domínguez, the technique was also applied by Remedios Varo, Hans Bellmer, and Max Ernst. I'm relating this technique to what I experienced reading Césaire: in his use of an exponential run-on of images wherein 3 or 4 separate levels are squared and yet continue to exist in constant movement. p. 188

as I reach your "equable casuarinas"—West Indian trees whose twigs resemble a cassowary's feathers. p. 189

of your "open letter" to the "local Catholic prelate"—"Césaire spoke out against collaboration most conspicuously in an 'open letter' to a local Catholic prelate who had attempted, in a pastoral communication, to exculpate the Catholic Church from complicity in the racialist politics of the Third Reich. What sparked the confrontation between the Bishop and the poet was a courageous public lecture (delivered in Martinique at Césaire's invitation) by René Etiemble with the pointed title 'The Opposition between Vichy Ideology and French Thought.' Like the rest of Césaire's prose, the defense of his friend Etiemble—a devastating critique, among other oppressions, of the connivance of the Church in negro slavery—is laced with apt historical documentation and well-chosen citations, and written in a vivid, arresting style that employs pungent irony. As an exposé of Western hypocrisy, it antipates the fulgurance of the author's later masterpiece, *Discourse on Colonialism*."—Gregson Davis, *Aimé Césaire*, Cambridge University Press, 2008. p. 190

<u>who stood at the top of the great teocalli</u>—"Pizarro before Cuzco" commanding "helmets" & lances & "cupidities". (All quoted language in these lines extracted from Césaire's Discourse.) p. 191

<u>or from comfortable means provided by assent</u>—In 2005 Césaire rejected the visit of Nicolas Sarkozy to Martinique when the latter was campaigning to show the postive side of French Colonialism. p. 191

<u>Queen Blanche of Castillo</u>—An example from the *Cahier* of the kind of irrelevant information forced down the gullet into children of colour during the midst of colonial education. p. 194

<u>when you spoke of eyes put out in Madagascar</u>—An approximate phrase extracted from the *Discourse*. p. 195

9—The number which is the threshold to the beyond. p. 196

<u>So when the ozone thins Aimé</u>—The unthinkable collapse of the present weather system on Earth. p. 196

<u>making contact with billions of habitable Earth zones</u>—Astrophysicist Alan Boss at the Carnegie Institute in Washington, D.C., estimates that there are 100 billion habitable planets in the visible universe. Our local star group contains 54 galaxies of which the Milky Way is a member. There are known to be numerous habitable planets within a half dozen light years from our Sun. p. 197

<u>BA</u>—In Egypt, the BA was the "breath of life: Eternal Invisible energy that runs through all visible functions—Essence of all things." p. 197

<u>where "no superior power" exists "beyond man"</u>—Words in quotes are taken from Clinical Psychologist Naim Akbar who is describing the Euro-American psychology, which contends in the main that there is no source of life beyond the observable. p. 199

(Louis) <u>Aragon</u>—The former confidant of Breton, having lost his imaginal radiance, becomes a cultural watchdog as a Communist bureaucrat.

He, in essence, argues for poetry which rises no higher than the literal so that language is made available to the masses. Césaire, on the other hand, bristles at this abyss of the imagination. Césaire's opposition, for all intents and purposes, seems to have carried the day as can be observed from the posture of our times.   p. 199

(Maurice) Thorez—One of Césaire's crowning moments was when he broke ties with the French Communist Party in 1956. His letter to Maurice Thorez was a testament to an uncommon courage within the circumstances of the times. Thorez, who was at the time the General Secretary of the French Communist Party, had not acknowledged "Khrushchev's revelations concerning Stalin," nor had the French Communists come close to making comment on the racial issues concerning the colonial pantheon held up by the Europeans. Césaire snapped the thread. "Césaire thus treats his break with the Communists as a declaration of independence and reclamation of initiative on the part of Black people. He ends with provocative thoughts on the relationship between universalism and particularism." (socialtext.dukejournals.org)   p. 199

"Phoronidea"—"A small group of…marine animals of uncertain systemic position."   p. 207

"amphisbaena"—Limbless lizards in the tropics, which have concealed eyes and ears, giving the impression that both its head and its tail exists as two heads.   p. 207

"in the colocasia meadows"—Asiatic and Polynesian plants "having the spadix terminated by a club-shaped or subulate appendage." It is a small genus.   p. 207

Miranda—"Miranda or Uranus V is the smallest and innermost of Uranus's five round satellites…" It "has one of the most extreme and varied topographies of any object in the Solar System."—Wikepedia.   p. 208

"Olmec incunabula"—La Venta, the heartland of Olmec civilization, is also home of the African stone heads with Africoid features, first found in 1862, which reveals an African appearance too obvious to miss. "They have Ethiopean-type braids." One in particular "has the circular ear-plug and incised decorative parallel lines found on other colossal Nubian heads in the Egyptian seaport in Tanis," giving proof of an African presence in Mexico almost "3000 years ago." The decoration on the heads are "uncannily similar" to leather helmets worn by the Egyptian-

Nubian military in the era of the Ramessids (Egyptian Pharoah) in the first millenium B.C. p. 212

<u>Po Tolo</u>—According to the Dogon, the most important star in the heavens.
p. 213

<u>Christophe</u>—Césaire's play, The Tragedy of King Christophe, is concerned with the poisonous nature of power, which consumed Christophe. In the early days of Haitian independence, Christophe became a major link in the perpetual weakening of Haiti's revolution. p. 218

<u>Caillois</u>—Roger Caillois, the Obliques French sociologist, was taken to task by Césaire for his non acknowledgment of the African contribution to humanity. By the middle of the 1940's "he sought to foster culture as the bulwark of Western civilization." Add to this a small antecdote about Caillois: while employed at UNESCO, he always failed to recognize his colleague, the great Congolese poet Tchicaya U Tam'si (1931-1988), who at one point had been associated, as had Caillois, with the Paris surrealists. p. 218

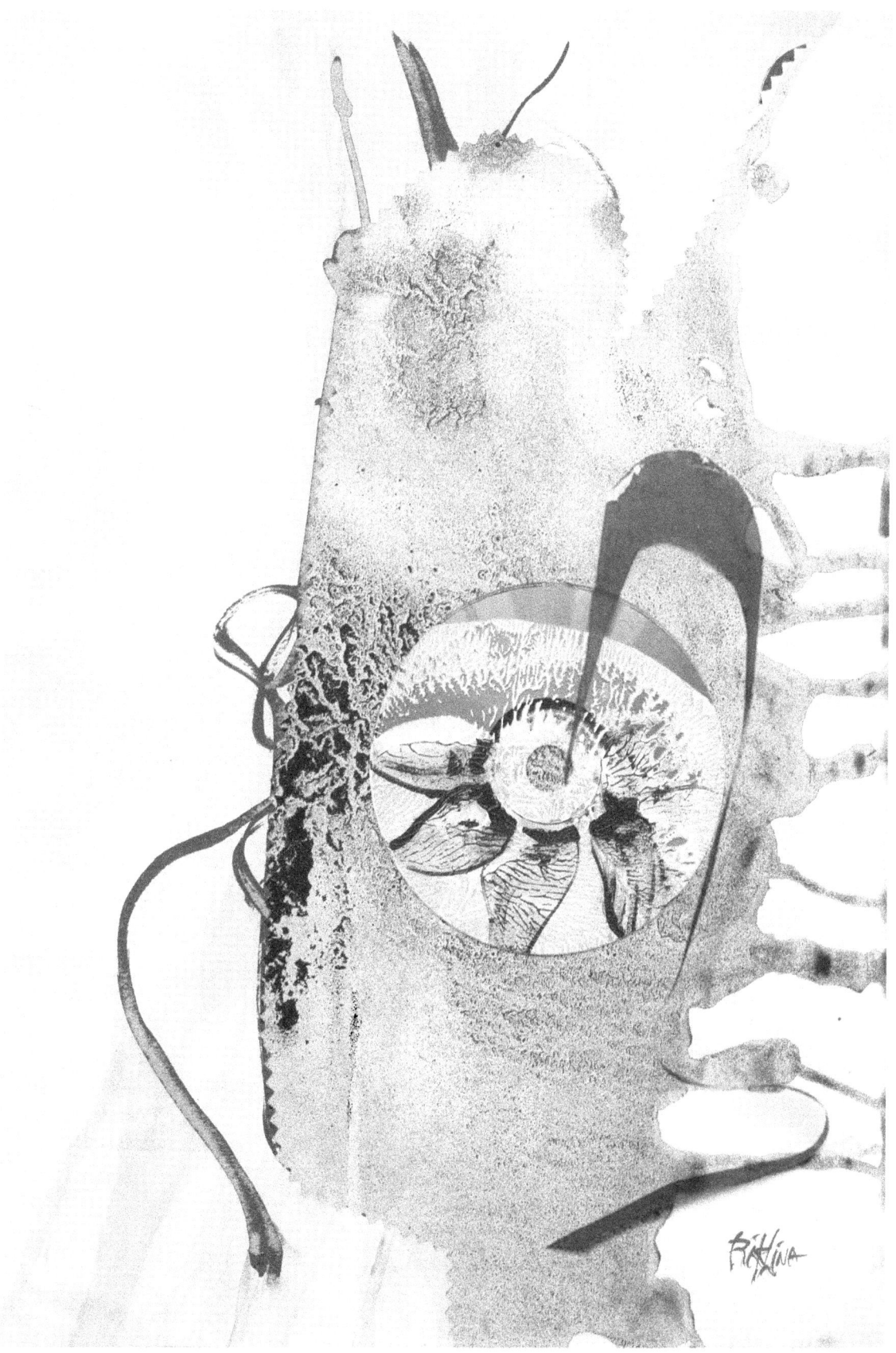

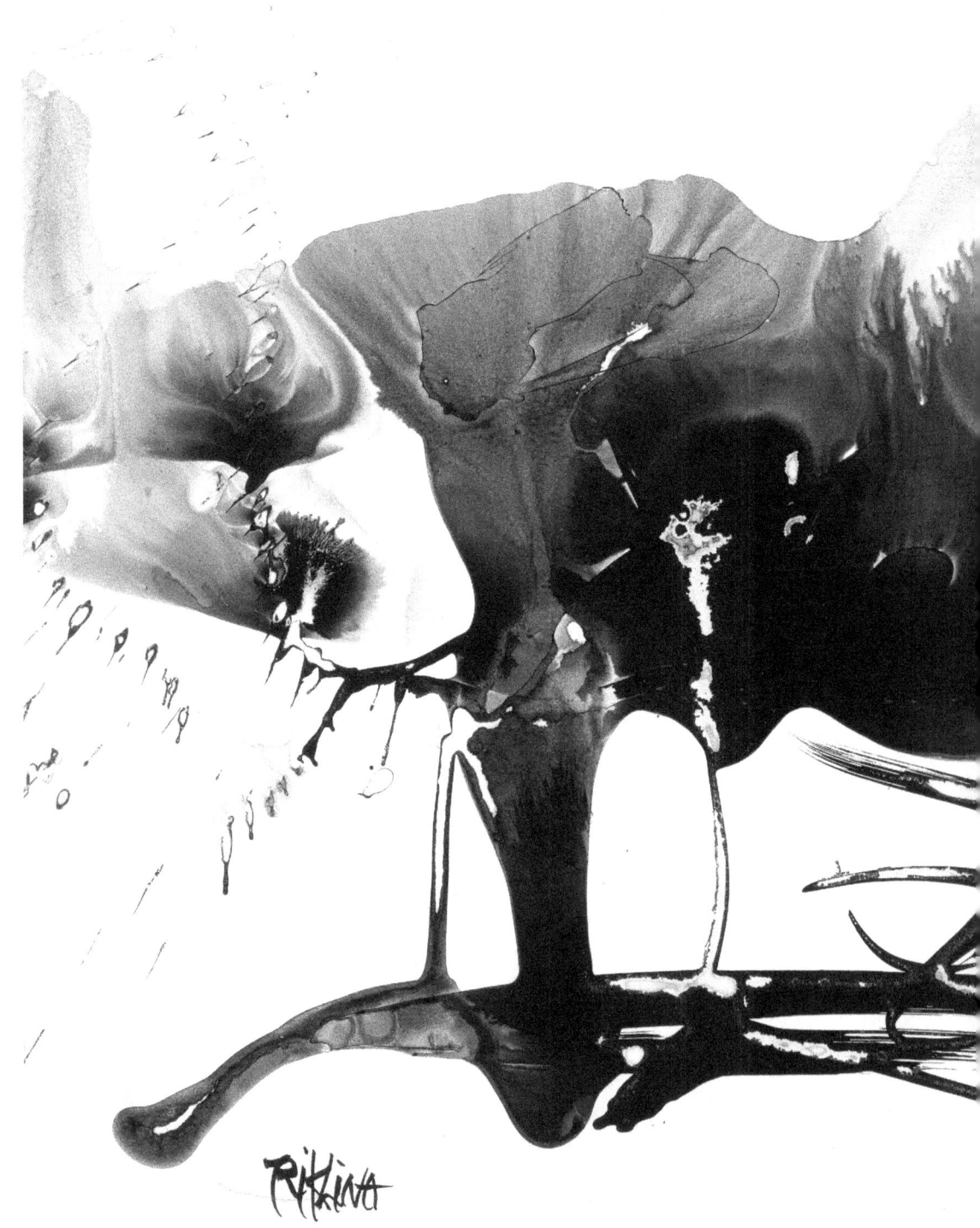

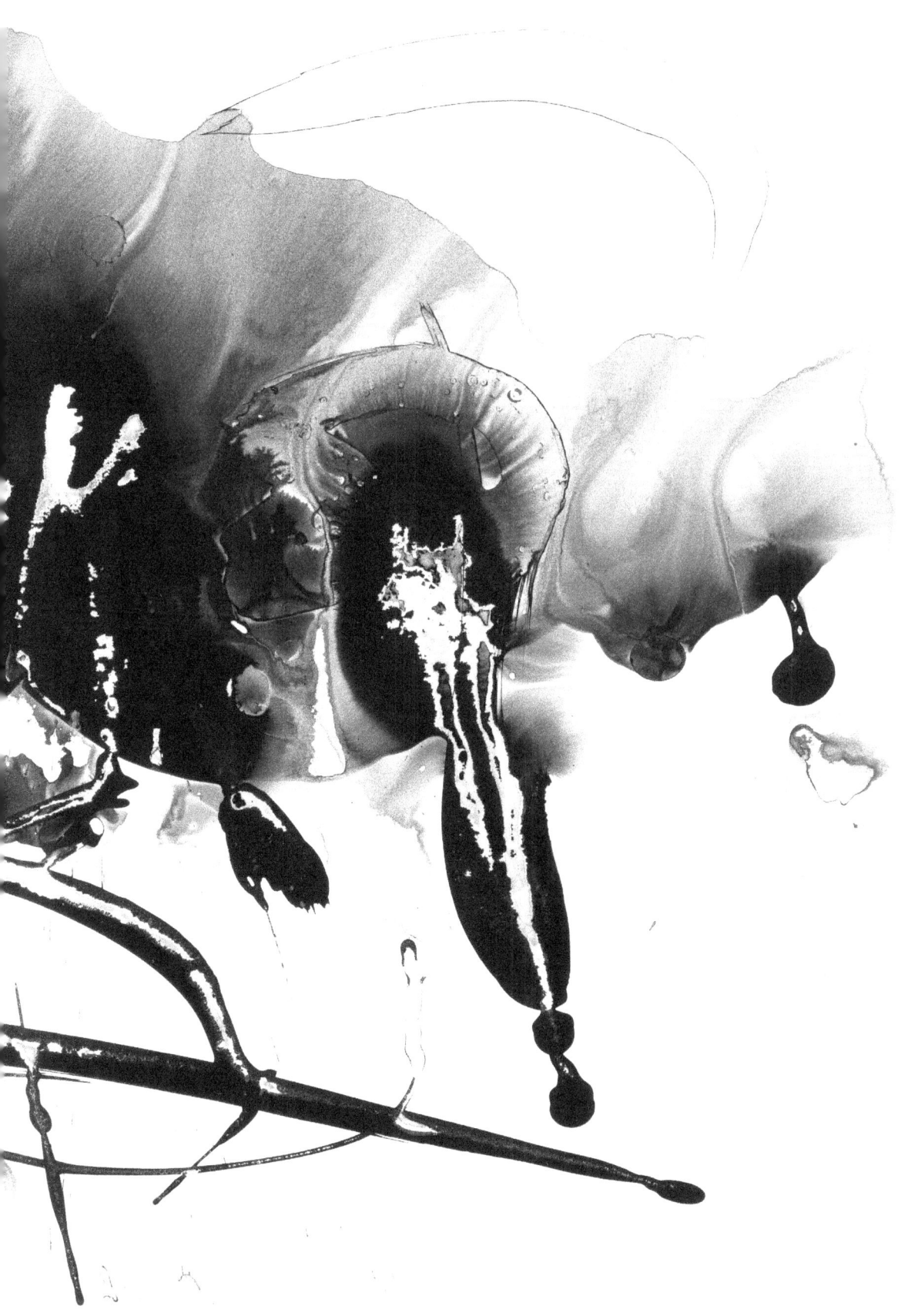

www.ingramcontent.com/pod-product-compliance
Lightning Source LLC
Chambersburg PA
CBHW080537170426
43195CB00016B/2595